Buddha's Table

Chat Mingkwan

Thai Feasting Vegetarian Style

Book Publishing Company
Summertown, Tennessee

Cover design: Warren Jefferson   Interior design: Gwynelle Dismukes
Food photos: Chat Mingkwan, Warren Jefferson   Food styling: Barbara Bloomfield
Some images © 2003-04 www.clipart.com   Props: Dave Fosdal

Published in the United States by
Book Publishing Company
P.O. Box 99
Summertown, TN 38483
1-888-260-8458

Pictured on the cover:
Pad Thai, pp. 117-119

Printed in Canada

ISBN 1-57067-161-3
ISBN13 978-1-57067-161-6
11 10 09 08 07   6 5 4 3 2

Chat Mingkwan.
  Buddha's table : the easiest 99 authentic Thai vegetarian recipes with delicious results / by Chat Mingkwan.
      p. cm.
  Includes bibliographical references and index.
  ISBN 1-57067-161-3 (alk. paper)
  1. Vegetarian cookery. 2. Cookery, Thai. I. Title.

  TX837.C45235 2004
  641.5'636'09593--dc22

                    2004019322

The Book Publishing Co. is a member of Green Press Initiative. We have elected to print this title on paper with postconsumer recycled content and processed chlorine free, which saved the following natural resources:

43 trees
2,017 lbs of solid waste
15,707 gallons of water
3.784 lbs of greenhouse gases
30 million BTUs

For more information visit: www.greenpressinitiative.org. Savings calculations thanks to the Environmental Defense Paper Calculator at www.papercalculator.org

Contents

*Again and again, Pia, you have changed me,
calmed me, and kept me grounded.*

Kop Khun!!!

A portion of the proceeds from this book will be donated to projects that promote the preservation of endangered wildlife. With your help, they'll keep on roaming.

FOREWORD

My first book, *The Best of Regional Thai Cuisine*, has received such a warm welcome that it is now in its second edition. Thank you all for your support.

For the past two years after the success of my first book, I have taken on a personal challenge: to convert all my recipes to vegetarian while keeping them as delicious and authentic as the original recipes. I have pondered the reasons why people choose to become vegetarian—to improve their health, to avoid animal cruelty, and to conserve resources—and decided that all of these make sense. For a period of nine months I became a vegetarian. During this time I felt a strong bond of solidarity with other vegetarians, mostly because of the limited availability of vegetarian food. Vegetarianism has become an alternative eating style, based on a choice to take a few less of life's basic pleasures. After all rhyme and reason, why are we still eating meat? As human beings, I believe we are entitled to comfort and indulgence, and vegetarians should not have to be denied such joys. So another reason I modified my recipes was to give vegetarians the pleasure of eating Thai food.

I have added vegetarian cooking classes to my teaching curriculum. These classes have become popular with vegetarians who want to expand their repertoire and with meat eaters who want to eat light. The concept of six degrees of separation is in play here: eventually you will meet up with a vegetarian whom you will one day invite to your home for dinner. What better way to show that you care than by cooking a vegetarian dish!

My students and vegetarian friends have been valuable resources, as they nudged and prodded me and offered their sincere critique. We have cooked and tasted each recipe over and over to ensure that they all are flawless and delicious, and, most important, that they manifest the Thai soul.

I am now confident enough to share these recipes with you and I humbly urge you to give them a try. Cooking should be a joyful experience, and I hope that these Thai recipes add diversity and pleasure to your life.

Sawasdee
Chat Mingkwan 2004

INTRODUCTION TO VEGETARIAN THAI CUISINE

Munksa-virut is a Sanskrit word that means "meatless." On holy days, Thai people visit local Buddhist temples and donate food and provisions to the monks in residence. In a holy ritual at day's end, the monks bestow the donors with health, prosperity, and tranquility, but ask them to adhere, at least for a day, to five simple rules for living a peaceful life. One of these rules is to refrain from killing all creatures, both large and small. By extension of this rule, Thai people eat vegetarian meals during these holy days.

One day before the full moon of the sixth month in 483 BC, Lord Buddha, anticipating his fate, summoned his closest disciples to what would be his final meal. He observed that some of the food donations were comprised of such low-quality ingredients as tough, fatty meats, and that if consumed, would harm his disciples. He chose instead to consume a large portion of these undesirable meats himself, thereby contracting a grave digestive illness that resulted in his death the next morning. Hearing this poignant story, a number of Buddha's followers, who represent a majority of Thai people, have committed themselves to living a healthy lifestyle, becoming vegetarian, and adhering to this simple rule: do not kill.

For many centuries, Thai vegetarian chefs and home cooks have modified their meals to include only plant-based ingredients. Through numerous years of trading with their Chinese and Indian neighbors, Thai people have been greatly influenced by their neighbors' diets and incorporated elements—such as soybean sauces, spices, and curries—into their own recipes. Over time, Thai vegetarian cuisine has expanded in its range of tastes, flavors, and textures, and more new dishes have been created to please the Thai palate. Consequently, Thai vegetarian dishes have acquired the same degree of complexity of flavors, textures, and colors as Thai meat dishes. But, unlike the latter, the vegetarian dishes are healthier, more economical, and do not require the killing of animals.

Thailand is divided into four regions: North, Northeast, Central, and South. They differ in geography, climate, dialect, and especially cuisine. The North region is situated on the high plateau among mountain ranges. Its cooler climate, compared to the other Thai regions, produces unique fruits and vegetables, such as longan. The neighboring countries of Myanmar and Laos influence the North culinary tradition. A meal called *Khun toke* is a classical style of dinner, showcasing the northern hospitality. The Northeast region is generally subjected to the mercy of nature. The majority of its farmland depends solely on the right amount of rain to enrich its poor soil, and it often endures droughts and floods. Its people are highly resourceful, adjusting to the extreme conditions. Northeast cuisine reflects the creativity and simplicity of making the best use of local ingredients. Laos, the neighboring country, has tremendous influence over the northeastern daily life, which is reflected in their language, art, architecture, and cuisine. *Pa khao lang* is the traditional meal of the northeastern hospitality. The Central region is blessed with fertile lands and plentiful crops. The capital city, Bangkok, is the economic, political, and cultural center. Food of the Central region has often been modified to fit ever-changing trends, borrowing or combining cuisines of other regions and foreign countries. It frequently reinvents itself to keep up with the demands of challenging new tastes, utilizing the influx of innovative ingredients and techniques. The South region is located a little above the equator on the peninsula stretching between the Gulf of Thailand and the Indian Ocean. The six-month local rainy season produces unique ingredients for the southern cuisine. Malaysia, bordering the south of Thailand, has a strong, predominantly Muslim influence over the beliefs and cuisine of the South. To learn more about different regional cuisines in Thailand, please read *The Best of Regional Thai Cuisine*, a cookbook that concentrates on this subject.

Buddha's Table is a collection of the most successful Thai recipes in terms of taste and execution for the home cook, and they all have been adjusted to please the Western vegetarian palate. Each of these recipes has been tested by several students of Thai, who, like you, seek exotic tastes and flavors and have discovered that there is no limit to vegetarian cooking. By using these recipes and the guidelines in this book, you, too, can cook delicious, healthy, beautiful Thai meals right in your own kitchen.

Characteristics of Thai Food

What makes food distinctively Thai? The answer is its characteristics: tasty, spicy, flavorful, colorful, fresh, and healthy. Keeping Thai food colorful, fresh, and healthy is easily achieved by selecting the right colors and the freshest, most healthful ingredients. But to capture the tasty, spicy, and flavorful—the essence of Thai—requires some research and familiarization.

Certain herbs and spices—such as lemongrass, galangal, and kaffir lime—provide enough flavors and aromas to make Thai cooking unique, and these flavors may vary in intensity, depending on the combination of ingredients used. Nowadays, fresh, frozen, preserved, and dried Thai herbs and spices, including such plant-based seasonings as sweet soy sauce and palm sugar, are found in local Asian grocery stores and even in well-stocked supermarket chains in many cities in the United States. These herbs and spices are used either raw (uncooked) or by infusing their essence into the food. For example, lemongrass can be eaten raw by slicing just the tender portions into fine pieces and adding them to salads or curry pastes, or it can be lightly crushed and cooked in a soup broth to infuse the soup with its flavor.

By tasting and eating Thai food often, you can become acquainted with, and develop a taste for, the flavors of popular dishes. In the following chapter, herbs, spices, fruits, vegetables, seasonings, and special ingredients are discussed, including easy ways to use them optimally in Thai cooking.

Eating Thai-Thai

The first "Thai" in "Thai-Thai" means freedom, as in the spirit of the Thai people, whose independence has been maintained throughout the centuries against formidable Western powers of colonization. The second "Thai" means Thai food and style. Eating anything, anytime, and anywhere seems to best capture the meaning of "eating Thai-Thai." And why can't we cook a delicious Thai meal our way, the vegetarian way?

Adapting to Western nomenclature, Thai food can be categorized as appetizer, soup, salad, main course, and dessert. But in reality, all dishes except desserts are served simultaneously and can be eaten in any order. Rice is an essential component of every meal, and there always is plenty of it—steamed white rice, glutinous sweet rice, or rice porridge, depending on the region and the meal. A Thai meal traditionally consists of several dishes with an assortment of flavors: sweet, hot, sour, and salty. Two to three types of cooking are used to provide a variety of tastes and textures. A typical meal includes a sharp-flavored salad and plenty of fresh vegetables; a soup, including curry dishes; a stir-fry vegetable; a deep-fried dish, such as fried potatoes and bananas; and a *namprik* (basic sauce or chili dip) with a side dish of vegetables. The dessert is made with a sweet base of coconut or a variety of seasonal fruits.

A one-dish meal, such as a noodle soup, fried rice, or curry and rice is quite popular for its convenience and quick preparation. But there always is an accompaniment of vegetables, sauces, or condiments. *Prik nam som* (chilies in vinegar) is as important for the noodle soup as *se-iew prik* (fresh chilies in soy sauce) is for the fried rice and *prik poan* (crushed dried chilies) is for those wanting extra heat.

Ingredients and Special Equipment for Thai Cooking

Ingredients for Thai Cooking

Most Thai dishes use fish sauce, primarily because of its saltiness and value as a flavor enhancer. Other exotic ingredients, such as shrimp paste and fermented fish, also add authentic flavors to Thai cuisine. But none of these products are vegetarian. Therefore, various plant-based seasonings are used instead.

Soy Products

Many types and brands of soy products make good alternatives to fish sauce, from light-colored soy sauce for cooking a white sauce to double-dark soy sauce for dark brown glazing. They also range in saltiness from low sodium (lite soy sauce) to those with a high salt content. There even is a sweet soy sauce made with a thick molasses and soy mixture. Instead of using animal products, a stir-fry soy sauce made from mushroom extract and a variety of soy pastes can easily replace the oyster sauce in stir-fry dishes. Black or yellow fermented beans and fermented tofu lend pungent, authentic flavors to a vegetarian dish and can be used in place of shrimp paste and fermented fish. These products are described in detail in the section that follows.

Nowadays, thanks to creative vegetarian chefs and merchants, innovative vegetarian foods with various tastes, textures, and colors occupy supermarket shelves. In addition to traditional products, seasoned tofu is made to simulate the flavor, texture, and appearance of such meat products as chicken, beef, pork, smoked duck, goose liver, and more. Products from the rivers and oceans, such as water plants and sea vegetables (seaweeds), replicate fish and seafood ingredients. Some of these products need a little getting used to as they are considered acquired tastes. For those who want to understand the very basics of food preparation, making your own tofu can be a fun and fulfilling project. (For a recipe for homemade tofu, see page 18.) You can make tofu from an assortment of beans and create diverse flavors and textures to produce a wide variety of dishes.

Soybean or Soya Bean (*Glycine maximus*): The Chinese have cultivated soybeans for centuries, dating back to 2838 BC. In China, they are considered one of the five sacred grains, *wu lu*. The United States has now become the largest producer of soybeans, supplying about 75 percent of the world's total production. There are more than one thousand varieties, ranging in size from a small pea to a large cherry. The beans come in various colors and combinations of red, yellow, green, brown, and black. They grow in pods that have fine, tawny hairs. Unlike other legumes, the soybean is low in carbohydrates and high in protein. Soybean products are also a good source of iron and contain vitamins B_1 and B_2 and linoleic acid, an essential oil that is one of the omega-3 fatty acids. Soybeans are used to produce kecap (Indonesian sweet and thick soy sauce), miso (see "soybean paste," page 15), natto (Japanese fermented beans), okara (the residue from soymilk), soybean oil, soy cheese, soy flour, soy ice cream, soy margarine, soy mayonnaise, soymilk, soy nuts, soy sauce, soy sour cream, soy yogurt, tamari (Japanese dark soy sauce), tofu, yuba (tofu sheets or skins), and soy pizza. Dried soybeans should be presoaked like any other dried beans before being cooked and used in soups, stews, casseroles, or other dishes. Bean sprouts grown from soybeans can be used in salads or as a cooked vegetable. Green soybeans (also called "edamame") are those picked when they are fully grown but not fully mature. They are sold fresh or frozen and come in their pods, which are bright green and covered with fuzz. Steam the pods for twenty minutes and serve them as a snack or appetizer. They can be shelled and eaten just like peanuts.

Bean Sauce and Bean Paste: These soy products are seasonings made from fermented soybeans. They can range from thin to thick and from smooth to chunky. They should be stored in a nonmetallic, tightly sealed container in the refrigerator for up to one year.

Black Bean Sauce is a thin, salty, full-flavored mixture made with mashed, fermented black soybeans and flavored with garlic and sometimes star anise.

Hot Black Bean Sauce has a medium consistency and is a combination of black soybeans, chilies, garlic, sesame oil, and sugar.

Brown Bean Sauce or Fermented Yellow Bean Sauce is thick and made with fermented, whole yellow soybeans, salt, and water.

Fermented Black Beans, also known as "Chinese black beans" or "salty black beans," are a Chinese specialty consisting of small black soybeans that have been preserved in salt before being packed into cans or plastic bags. They have an extremely pungent, salty flavor and must be soaked in warm water for about thirty minutes before using. Store, tightly covered, in the refrigerator for up to one year.

Soybean Paste, called *miso*, is essential in Japanese cooking. It has the consistency of peanut butter and comes in a wide variety of flavors and colors. This fermented soybean paste has three basic categories: barley miso, rice miso, and soybean miso. Each has a different salt content and some have added sugar. Miso can be used in sauces, soups, marinades, main dishes, and salad dressings. Stored in an airtight container in the refrigerator, it should keep several months.

Sweet Bean Paste is made with fermented soybeans and sugar. It is quite thick and has a sweet-salty flavor.

Soymilk: *Nam tao hu* is an iron-rich liquid made by pressing ground, cooked soybeans. It has more protein than cow's milk. Soymilk is a cholesterol-free, nondairy product and is low in calcium, fat, and sodium. It makes an excellent alternative to cow's milk for vegetarians. Soymilk has a tendency to curdle when mixed with acidic ingredients, such as lemon juice or wine. It is an important ingredient in making tofu.

Ingredients

Soy Sauce: *Se-iew* is a dark, salty sauce made with fermented, boiled soybeans and roasted wheat or barley. China and Japan produce a number of varieties ranging in color from light to dark and in texture from thin to very thick.

Dark Soy Sauce is the "regular" soy sauce. It has a rich soy flavor and color. This soy sauce is generally used when a particular type is not specified in a recipe.

Double-Dark Soy Sauce is a lot darker than regular soy sauce and is used mostly for glazing and for sauces that need a dark brown color.

Fermented Bean Curds *Tao hu yee* are tofu curds that have been fermented with salt, water, vinegar, rice wine, and/or spices until they develop an extremely pungent taste and flavor equivalent to Thai shrimp paste or Limburger cheese. They come in a small jar and may be stored, tightly sealed, in the refrigerator for up to one year.

Fermented Yellow Beans *Tow jiew* are whole yellow beans that have been fermented in water and salt. They often come in a bottle and are ready to be used in stir-fries and sauces. Close the lid tightly and store in the refrigerator for one year.

Light Soy Sauce *Se-iew kow* is much thinner and lighter but saltier than regular dark soy sauce. It is also called "cooking soy sauce," as it has less soy flavor and a lighter color that won't turn sauces dark brown. Light soy sauce is the best substitute for fish sauce in a vegetarian dish.

Lite Soy Sauce is regular soy sauce with less sodium.

Sushi or Sashimi Soy Sauce is a milder soy sauce with added rice products to sweeten its taste. It is more expensive than regular soy sauce and often is used as a dipping sauce.

Sweet Soy Sauce *Se-iew wan* is a thick, sweet, dark sauce made from soy sauce and molasses. It often is used instead of sugar and is valued for its dark color, thick texture, and sweetness.

Tamari is the Japanese dark soy sauce. It is rich, thick, and extremely dark.

Tofu or Bean Curd: *Tao hu* is made from curdled soymilk, resulting in curds that are drained and pressed in a fashion similar to making cheese. Tofu has a bland, slightly nutty flavor that easily takes on the flavor of the food it's cooked with. Tofu comes in regular, low-fat, and nonfat varieties, and in textures ranging from soft to extra firm.

Baked Tofu *Tao hu oop* is baked tofu in a sealed package. Baking rids it of most moisture, making the tofu extra dry and firm with an intense flavor. It is often prepared with added spices, such as Chinese five-spice. Store it in the refrigerator for up to one week.

Fried Tofu *Tao hu tod* is deep-fried tofu in a sealed package. It is semi-crunchy on the outside and soft and smooth on the inside. It contains small air pockets that readily absorb sauces and flavors. Store it in the refrigerator for up to one week.

Pressed Tofu *Tao hu kang* is sold in small squares. It has a "meaty," chewy texture and may have added coloring or flavorings.

Silken Tofu *Tao hu oon*, named for its silky smooth texture, comes in soft, regular, and firm styles. It usually is packed in water and is sold in a sealed, plastic container. It also may be vacuum-packed in plastic without water. Silken tofu also is available in aseptically sealed packages that may be stored unopened at room temperature for up to eight months. Once opened, silken tofu should be stored in water, which should be changed daily. The cakes should be kept refrigerated for no more than one week.

Tofu Sheets or Tofu Skins *Phong tao hu* are a thin layer of tofu that curdles on the surface of hot soymilk. They are sold three different ways: fresh; folded or rolled in a sealed plastic package and dried in a big sheet; or packed airtight in a plastic bag. Dried tofu sheets can be kept for up to one year and must be reconstituted before using. Fresh tofu sheets will keep for about one week in the refrigerator. Fresh or reconstituted dried tofu sheets can be cut to desired sizes and used as wrappers or additions to soups and stir-fries.

Ingredients

Homemade Tofu

Tao Hu

Either soybeans or yellow mung beans can be processed to make tofu. The soybean or soya bean (*Glycine maximus*) was domesticated in China by the third millennium BC. The soybean has many varieties that differ in seed size and color, including white, green, red, brown, and black. The most common kind is smallish and pale brown and is known in Indian cuisine as *white gram*. The mung bean, on the other hand, is the seed of the plant *Vigna radiata*, a native of India. It is known as *golden gram* or *green gram*, depending on its color, and is often used as a main ingredient in the Indian dish "dal." All varieties of mung beans, after being shelled and split, have a small, pale yellow seed inside. The Chinese regularly use mung beans to grow bean sprouts, which are different from soya or soybean sprouts, and as a source of starch for mung bean vermicelli or cellophane or glass noodles. Dried soybeans and mung beans are sold already hulled (the pod has been removed) and are available whole or split.

Soybeans or yellow mung beans are soaked in water for three hours before they are processed (blended with water) and the liquid is extracted for "milk." Both firm and soft tofu can be made from soybean or mung bean milk. To make firm tofu, magnesium sulfate is added to the bean milk; to make soft tofu, calcium sulfate is added. The firmness also depends on how much whey (the liquid that remains after the solids have been coagulated) has been extracted. Without magnesium or calcium sulfate, a thicker milk with more bean pulp is required, along with using not-too-fine cheesecloth to strain the processed blend. The pulp will help solidify the mixture, but it will only make a soft tofu after more water has been squeezed (pressed) out. The tofu will be very crumbly; handle it carefully.

Square or rectangular wooden or plastic frames are used in commercial tofu making to form the tofu. For homemade tofu, large, round cookie cutters, empty aluminum cans cut open at both ends, or small, square milk cartons cut open at both ends can be used as the frames.

Makes 6 servings

1 pound dried soybeans or yellow mung beans
1/2 gallon hot water
Flavorings or spices, such as salt, soy sauce, or Chinese five-spice (optional)
1 tablespoon magnesium sulfate or calcium sulfate (optional)

Soak the beans in hot water to cover for 2–3 hours or until the beans have swelled and fully absorbed the water.

Combine one-third of the beans with some of the soaking water in a blender and process until the beans are well puréed. Place a strainer on top of a medium pot and line the strainer with fine cheesecloth. Pour the mixture into the cheesecloth and pull the cloth's edges together. Squeeze as much soymilk out of the mixture as possible and discard the solids. Continue processing the remainder of the soaked beans in a similar fashion.

Put the pot over medium heat and bring the soymilk to a boil. Boil for about 3 minutes, stirring constantly. Add any optional flavorings at this point. Remove from the heat and let cool for 10 minutes or until lukewarm. Slowly stir in the optional magnesium or calcium sulfate to help the soymilk curds congeal. Let the tofu sit undisturbed for 5–7 minutes or until lightly firm.

Place a rack on a baking sheet and place four 4 x 4 x 2-inch or 3 x 5 x 2-inch frames over the rack. Line the frames with 8 x 8-inch or 6 x 10-inch fine cheesecloth. Alternatively, place several large cookie cutters or homemade frames made from aluminum cans or milk cartons on the rack and line with oversized fine cheesecloth. Scoop the tofu into the cheesecloth to overfill the frames and fold the edges of the cheesecloth to completely wrap the tofu. Place flat heavy objects (such as a piece of brick in a zippered plastic bag) on top of the tofu for 10–15 minutes (or until it is at your desired firmness) to squeeze out more water and make the tofu firmer. Steam the wrapped tofu on a rack over boiling water until it is completely heated through, about 5 minutes. Let cool and unwrap the tofu for further use. Store the tofu by submerging it in cold water. It will keep refrigerated for up to five days (be sure to change the water daily).

Other Ingredients Essential to Thai Cuisine

Thai food is characterized by the four tastes: sweet, sour, hot, and salty. The Thais frequently use palm sugar for sweet, lime and tamarind for sour, chilies for hot, and fish sauce (or soy sauce) for salty. Some of the ingredients are new to Western kitchens, though they are accessible through Asian markets in the United States. Don't be put off by unfamiliar ingredients and techniques. Thai cooking is not a difficult or complicated process. In fact, by becoming familiar with the ingredients and their uses, lovers of Thai food can easily prepare any dish on a Thai menu. Only ingredients that are unfamiliar to the Western kitchen are mentioned in this chapter, including where to find and how to use them.

Herbs and Spices

What makes Thai food unique is the special herbs and spices. The ingredients and cooking methods from neighboring countries have greatly influenced Thai cuisine. Thais have adopted noodles from the Chinese to create the classic dish *Pad Thai* (page 117). Curries from India have filtered into Thai households and been modified for Thai tastes. Surprisingly, from as far away as Central America, chilies have traveled on Spanish and Portuguese fleets to land on fertile Thai soil and become part of the signature spicy Thai dishes. These herbs and spices usually grow in tropical climates and find their way to Western countries. Nowadays, fresh Thai herbs and spices can be produced in the United States, especially in the hot climates of Florida and Hawaii, and in California during the summer months. As the popularity of Thai and Southeast Asian cuisine grows, so does the market for these popular herbs and spices. Thai sweet basil and bird's-eye chilies earn their shelf spaces commercially in the big-name grocery stores.

As the weather permits, I cultivate my own Thai herb garden. Some of the herbs do well in the ground and some are very content in pots. Most nurseries now carry exotic herb seeds and starter plants for both cooking and decorative purposes. Most of the herbs are perennials and do very well in the ground during the hot months. The ones in pots can be conveniently moved indoors during severe weather and generally last for two to three years. Though most Thai herbs and spices can be cultivated locally, some must be imported in various forms: fresh, dried, powdered, frozen, and canned in brine. For some herbs and spices, substitutions can easily be made by using items more readily available outside Thailand. However, to maintain an authentic essence, the herbs and spices with an asterisk (*) cannot be replaced.

Basil: Three kinds of basil are used in Thai cooking. At a very young age, I first learned to cook by identifying their different flavors, appearances, and uses. If I was sent to the market, I often came back with all three kinds of basil to avoid making a mistake. It may be hard to find the exact basil to use. You can alternate among them or just use Italian basil.

> **Holy Basil** *Bai kaprow (Ocimum sanctum)* has a distinctive light violet-reddish hue on both its leaves and stems. It imparts a mint-like zesty and spicy flavor and is used for stir-fries such as *Pad Kaprow* (page 112). Holy basil is hard to find and is mostly available during the midsummer months, when it thrives.

> **Lemon Basil** *Bai mangluk (Ocimum carnum)* has light green leaves with a slight speckle of hairs, green stems, and sometimes white flowers. It has a nippy peppery and lemon flavor that goes well with soups and salads, especially with *kanom jeen* curry noodles.

> **Thai Sweet Basil** *Bai horapha (Ocimum basilicum)* has small, flat, green leaves with pointy tips, and its stems and flowers are sometimes reddish purple. It imparts a very intense taste with a strong anise or licorice flavor. It's often used as a flavorful garnish for coconut curries and leafy vegetables. Ordinary sweet basil makes a good substitute. Thai sweet basil is available year-round.

Cardamom:* *Luk kravan (Elettaria cardamomum)* is indigenous to India and Sri Lanka. Cardamom has a eucalyptus-like lemony flavor and is essential to Thai *Massamun Curry* (page 142). It is available as dried whole seeds or ground.

Chili: *Prik khee nu* is the smallest and hottest kind of Thai chili; the same words are often used to refer to something that is small but powerful. For example, in Thai boxing, a small but capable boxer with odds and size against him is dubbed *lek prik khee nu*, which means he has much tenacity and a chance to win. For chilies, the smaller ones indicate more heat.

> **Bird's-Eye or Thai Chilies** *Prik khee nu suan (Capsicum minimum)*, literally "mouse droppings," are the smallest chilies. They are red or green and have an extremely pungent taste. Bird's-eye chilies are used for chili sauces and dips and are added to curry pastes for spicy heat. They are available in most Asian grocery stores under the label "Thai chilies." See photo, facing page 32.

> **Prik Chee Fa** *(Capsicum frutescens)* come in red, yellow, or green and are the size of a forefinger. They look similar to a jalapeño but with a pointy tip. They are a lot milder than the bird's-eye chilies and are used both fresh and dried. Fresh green chilies are used in Thai green curry paste. Dried red chilies, *prik haeng*, are used in Thai red and yellow curry paste. If fresh *prik chee fa* are not available, use fresh serrano or jalapeño chilies. For the dried chilies, large dried Mexican chilies, such as guajillo chilies, California chilies, or New Mexico chilies, are good substitutes.

> **Serrano** *(Capsicum annum)* are green chilies with smooth skin and round bodies. As they mature, their color changes from bright green to scarlet red, then yellow. They are easily found in markets in the United States. Their flavor is as mild as the *prik chee fa*, making them a good multipurpose chili.

Chinese Five-Spice: This is a Chinese ground spice mixture, also sold as "five-fragrance powder." It is golden brown in color and consists of star anise, fennel, cloves, cassia (Asian cinnamon), and Sichuan pepper (or ginger and/or cardamom). The flavor of star anise is the strongest in the mixture.

Cilantro:* *Phak chee (Coriandrum sativum)*, or Chinese parsley, is indispensable to Thai cooking and is used generously. Each part of the plant, from the roots to the leaves, can be utilized for different purposes. The roots and seeds (also known as "coriander seeds") are very pungent and are important ingredients in curry pastes and for flavoring clear soup broth. The stems and leaves are used both for flavoring and as a leafy green garnish. Cilantro has delicate, light green leaves and stems with white or light pink flowers, which are all edible. In most supermarkets in the United States, cilantro is sold without roots, but the stems can be substituted for the roots in cooking. To enhance their aroma, coriander seeds should be dry-roasted before being used in a recipe. Like any other dry spices, coriander seeds and ground coriander will lose their fragrance and flavor after six months.

Galangal:* *Kha (Alpinia officinarum)*, or *Siamese ginger*, is a perennial rhizome plant similar to ginger but with a larger and brighter colored root. The root tips are pink and have a strong medicinal taste, so it can't be eaten directly like ginger. Galangal is used as a pungent ingredient in ground curry pastes. Valued for its unique and exotic aroma, it is the main herb in the popular sweet-and-sour *Tom Yum* (page 93) and coconut galangal *Tom Kha* (page 89) soups. Galangal is available as the fresh root or in frozen, dried, and powdered forms in most Asian grocery stores. If using dried slices of galangal, soak them in warm water for at least thirty minutes, or until the pieces can bend easily, before putting them in a blender. If a substitution is needed, replace fresh galangal with half the amount of dried galangal called for in a recipe. Regular ginger cannot duplicate the authentic essence of galangal. Only as a last resource should ginger ever be used instead of galangal. See photo, facing page 32.

Garlic Chives: *Kui chay (Allium schoenoprasum)*, or Chinese chives, have a stronger aroma than European chives. They have long, flat, slender leaves and long stems topped with white flowers. They are used exclusively for stir-fry dishes, such as *Pad Thai* (page 117), and as a garnish over noodle dishes. Green onions are a good substitute.

Kaffir Lime:* *Magrood (Citrus hystrix)* has a thick, dark, wrinkled skin. Its glossy, dark green leaves, *bai magrood*, and rinds, *pew magrood*, are used for a strong citrus flavor in curry pastes, soups, and salads. They are available in Asian grocery stores in fresh, dried, and frozen forms. Fresh kaffir lime has a slightly bitter juice that is rarely used. See photo, facing page 32.

Jasmine: *Mali* are flowers of the Thai jasmine shrub. Their strong, sweet fragrance is often used in Thai desserts in the same manner as vanilla extract. Jasmine extract in a bottle is available at well-stocked Asian grocery stores. Jasmine water, *nam mali*, is made from floating a handful of flowers in a bowl of cold water overnight or diluting the extract with water. Use rose water or vanilla extract for a substitute.

Lemongrass:* *Ta-krai (Cymbopogon citratus)* resembles a grass and has a strong lemon aroma. To use lemongrass, cut off the grassy top and root end. Peel and remove the large, tough outer leaves of the stalk until you reach the light purple inner leaves. Chop it very finely for use in salads, grind it into curry pastes, or cut it into two-inch portions and bruise it to use in soup broth. Lemongrass can be found fresh in most grocery stores because it has a very long shelf life. Dried and frozen lemongrass also is available in most Asian stores. See photo, facing page 32.

Lesser Ginger:* *Kra-chai (Kaempferia pandurata)* is also a rhizome plant, another relative of the gingerroot but milder in flavor. Fresh *kra-chai* comes in tubes—long, thin, and fingerlike, with yellow meat and brown skin. It is a main ingredient for making a curry broth for *kanom jeen* noodles. Lesser ginger also is sold in jars with brine. See photo, facing page 32.

Pandan or Pandanus: *Bai taey*, or screw pine leaves *(Pandanus odoratissimus)*, are the long, slender, blade-like, dark green leaves of a tropical plant. They impart a sweet floral fragrance that is popular in Thai desserts. Their intense green color is valued as a natural food coloring. Pound and grind the leaves with a little water and strain the mixture to get a liquid extract. Bottled pandan extract is available in well-stocked Asian grocery stores. Thais use pandan instead of vanilla in their cooking. Use rose water or vanilla extract as a substitute.

Preserved Turnip: *Hau chai po*, or *Chinese pickled radish*, is a salt-cured Chinese turnip or radish. It is a flavor enhancer that is salty and sweet with a crunchy texture. Chop it into small chunks before using. It is available in the dried goods section of all Asian markets.

Tamarind:* *Ma-kham (Tamarindus indica)* is a fruit pod of a very large tamarind tree with fine, fernlike leaves. Fresh green tamarind, *ma-kham awn*, can be used in chili dips or pickled and served as a snack. The ripe brown pulp, *ma-kham paek*, is extracted for tamarind liquid, *nam ma-kham paek*, and is used to impart a sour flavor without the tartness of lime. The tamarind liquid often is used in soups and stir-fries. At the Asian grocery stores it is available in a pulp block, powdered, or ready-made in a jar. To make tamarind liquid from the pulp, soak a one-inch cube of tamarind with one-half cup of warm water. Work the tamarind with your fingers until it disintegrates and the water turns brown and thickens. Alternatively, boil the pulp with the water for 5–7 minutes or until it disintegrates. Strain the mixture through a sieve; it will make about one-third cup of tamarind liquid.

Turmeric:* *Kamin (Curcuma domestica)* is another rhizome plant that is bright yellow, making it good for both coloring and flavoring. Ground turmeric is used mainly in curry powders. Fresh turmeric is hard to find; dried or ground turmeric can be substituted.

Fruits and Vegetables

Baby Corn: *Khao phot awn (Zea mays)* is young corn that has been harvested before maturity. It is very sweet and tender and is used in stir-fries or as a fresh vegetable to accompany chili dips. Fresh baby corn is available in well-stocked

Asian produce markets, but cooked and canned baby corn is widely available. There is no comparison in taste between fresh and canned baby corn.

Bamboo Shoots: *Naw mai (Phyllostachys, Bambusa,* and *Dendrocalamus)* are the young sprouts of the bamboo bush. They have a neutral taste with a crunchy texture and absorb flavors well in various Thai dishes, especially curries. You can buy bamboo shoots fresh, cooked, or canned in Asian supermarkets. To prepare fresh bamboo shoots, trim the tips and remove the tough outer shell. Cut off the tough bottom ends. Boil the shoots with two or three changes of water, boiling each time for 3–5 minutes, until they are tender but still crunchy. See photo, facing page 32.

Banana Flower: *Hua plee* is the male part at the tip of a banana flower where the female counterpart at the end develops into the banana fruit. To prepare banana flower, remove the tough, red outer petals and trim back the stem. Cut it in half and cook (debitter) in boiling water for 5–7 minutes; then slice and add it to soups or salads. The flower also can be eaten raw as an accompaniment to a main dish. It needs to be soaked in water with lime or lemon juice or rubbed with a slice of lime to keep it from turning brown.

Bottle Gourd or Asian Gourd: *Boub (Lagenaria siceraria)* is a long, slender, green vegetable similar to a green zucchini. Sometimes its skin will be ripped and tough and the gourd will need to be peeled before it is cooked in stir-fry and curry dishes. Mature bottle gourds have a hard, dried shell that is water resistant and can be used as a bottle.

Chinese Broccoli: *Kana (Brassica oleracea)* or *gai lan* has dark green, leathery leaves that grow on thick stalks. Leaves, stalks, and flowers can be eaten. Peel the tough skin off the stalk before using. Regular broccoli is a good substitute.

Chinese Celery: *Kheun chai (Apium graveolens)* is smaller than Western celery and has a stronger flavor. It is served fresh in salads or cooked in clear broth. In traditional Thai cooking, it is used mostly in seafood dishes to counteract the fishy flavor.

Coconut: *Ma-prow (Cocos nucifera)* is the most versatile plant: its leaves and trunk are used in construction; the shell of the fruit is used for fiber and in the garment industry; and its fruit is used for food and in medicines. Coconut sugar, or palm sugar, is extracted from the sap of the coconut flower, and palm wine, or toddy, is further refined by fermentation and distillation.

> **Coconut Cream** *Hua krati* is the rich and creamy liquid from the first pressing of coconut milk.

> **Coconut Milk** *Kati* is derived from processing the grated white meat of the ripe brown coconut, not to be confused with the clear coconut water (the liquid inside the fruit). The process involves steeping the fresh-grated coconut meat in boiling water and letting it stand for 5–10 minutes before pressing it and straining out the thick white liquid. The first pressing usually is set aside for a rich coconut cream. The second and third pressings yield a less fatty coconut milk. In markets in the United States, you now can choose from many forms of ready-processed coconut milk and cream— fresh in a ripe coconut, frozen, powdered, in a milk carton, and canned. After standing on a shelf awhile, the canned coconut separates into a thick top layer of cream and a bottom layer of milk. By opening the can gently and scooping out the thick layer, you can obtain coconut cream. If you shake the can before opening it, you will get coconut milk.

> **Smoked Coconut** *Ma-prow pow* is a young, green coconut that has been smoked. This process intensifies its flavor, giving it a slightly smoky aroma and taste.

> **Young Coconut** *Ma-prow awn* is popular for the clear, refreshing, flavorful drink often served with tender white coconut meat.

Eggplant: *Ma-kheua* comes in many varieties: its size ranges from a small marble to a baseball; its shape may be oval to spherical; and its color extends from white to yellow to green to purple. Three varieties frequently are used in Thai cooking:

Long Eggplant *Ma-kheua yao* is a long green or purple fruit with a denser texture than regular purple eggplant. It is often used in salads and stir-fry and curry dishes.

Marble Eggplant *Ma-kheua puang (Solanum torvum)* grows in clusters. It is bright green in color and is the size of small marbles.

Thai Eggplant *Ma-kheau pro (Salanum melongena)* is the size of golf ball. It is light green with a crunchy texture. It is used as a vegetable in red or green curry and also is served as a fresh vegetable with a chili dip. See photo, facing page 32.

Jackfruit: *Kanon (Artocarpus heterophyllus)* is a very large fruit with spiky, brownish-green skin. Its meat is a brilliant yellow or orange and has a unique, sweet flavor. Jackfruit often is used in Thai desserts because of its neutral sweetness that goes with almost anything. In the United States, jackfruit canned in syrup is readily available in Asian grocery stores.

Jicama: *Mun jael (Pachyrhizus erosus)* is an underground tuber with crunchy, juicy, ivory-colored flesh and a sweet, bland flavor that suits everything from fruit cups to stir-fries. Jicama can be eaten raw or cooked after peeling its thin, matte, sandy-brown skin.

Kabocha: *Fuk thong (Cucurbita moschata)* is considered a winter squash in the United States. It has a jade-green rind with celadon-green streaks. When cooked, its pale orange flesh is tender, smooth, and sweet. Choose kabochas that are heavy for their size. The rind should be dull and firm; avoid any with soft spots. Kabochas are similar to pumpkins and acorn squash, and they are cooked the same way.

Lily Bud or Lily Flower: *Dok mai cheen (Hemerocallis fulva)* is the flower of a day lily that has been dried. It has a unique flavor with a sweet fragrance and elastic texture. Soak lily buds in warm water to soften them before using them in soups, salads, and stir-fries.

Longan: *Lumyai (Dimocarpus longan)* has been cultivated for centuries as the cash crop in the cool Northern region of Thailand. Longan fruit is round, the size of a cherry, with leathery brown skin, a very sweet flavor, and a strong, unique aroma. It can be eaten fresh and is often used as a main ingredient in Thai desserts. In the United States, imported canned longan can be found year-round. Fresh longan can be found seasonally in well-stocked Asian markets.

Long Bean: *Thua Fak Yao (Vigna unguiculata var sesquipedalis)*, also known as yard-long bean or snake bean, has slender, green or purple pods that grow up to twelve inches in length. They are excellent eaten raw or cooked in stir-fry dishes. Long beans are available in most supermarkets during the spring and summer months. Green beans are a good substitute.

Lychee: *Lin chee (Litchi chinensis)* fruit originated in China but also has been cultivated in Northern Thailand and has become a local fruit. Lychee fruit is round, a little bit bigger than a cherry, with red bumpy skin and a sweet flavor that has a pleasant sour hint. In the United States, imported canned lychee can be found year-round. Fresh lychee can be found seasonally in well-stocked Asian markets.

Morning Glory: *Phak bung (Ipomoea aquatica)*, also called *water spinach* or *swamp cabbage*, has roughly triangular-shaped leaves and hollow stems. The Thai variety has dark green leaves with red stalks, while the Chinese type is lighter green and has thicker stalks. The tender tips are popular for flambés or stir-fries, or they are eaten fresh as a side vegetable. Spinach is the closest substitute.

Pomelo: *Som oo (Citrus grandis)* is the giant grapefruit now readily available in almost all Asian markets in early winter. It is sweeter and less bitter than the local grapefruit and may be eaten either as a fruit or as a main ingredient in salad.

Papaya: *Malagor (Carica papaya)* usually is eaten ripe as a fresh fruit, but unripe green papaya is very popular for Thai green papaya salad. Choose a papaya that is very hard and firm with a bright green color. Peel and seed the papaya before shredding or cutting it into fine matchstick pieces. In the United States, green papaya that is imported from Mexico is available in well-stocked Asian grocery stores.

Rambutan: *Ngor (Nephelium lappaceum)* is a fruit with a distinctive, hairy red skin and sweet, opaque white meat. It is imported seasonally from Asia. However, *ngor* canned in syrup also is readily available.

Seaweed: *Sarai ta-lem (Ulva lactua)* is usually sold fresh in bulk in large, open crocks of water. It has been cleaned, trimmed, and processed, most commonly in the shape of a bowtie, knot, or string. It also is sold dried in packages and is usually reconstituted before using. Seaweed can be cooked in soups and stir-fries or poached before using in salads.

Water Chestnuts: *Haeo (Eleocharis dulcis)* add a sweet flavor and white crunchy texture to many dishes, especially desserts. They are the tuber of a plant in the sedge family and are round with black skin. Fresh water chestnuts are available in well-stocked Asian markets. Choose firm, unblemished ones. Peel off the black skin before using. Canned water chestnuts are available in all supermarkets. There is no comparison between fresh and canned water chestnuts.

Rice, Noodles, Wrappers, and Other Beans and Grains

Rice: *Khao (Oryza sativa)* is the steamed long-grain rice that accompanies almost every Thai meal.

> **Brown Rice** *Khao gong* is long-grain rice with only its inedible outer husk removed; it is not ground or polished into a smooth, white grain. The nutritious, high-fiber bran coating gives it a light tan color, nutty flavor, and chewy texture. Brown rice is subject to rancidity, which limits its shelf life to about six months. Brown rice or unmilled brown rice, now regarded as a health food, was rarely eaten in rice-staple countries, where people valued the whiteness and tenderness of the milled grains. The brown or reddish outer layers (bran) are rich in fiber and in the B-group vitamins. Cook brown rice the same way as regular white long-grain rice,

but add a little more water and increase the cooking time to about 40 minutes.

Fragrant Rice or Jasmine Rice *Khao hoam mali* is extremely popular and available almost everywhere. Before cooking, rinse the rice well with water to cleanse away any dirt and foreign objects. Cook the rice in a pot with a tight-fitting lid using a ratio of one part rice to two parts cold water. Bring to a boil. Reduce the heat, cover, and simmer for 15–20 minutes or until the water has been absorbed. Remove from the heat and let the rice stand, covered, for 10-15 minutes before serving. When rice is properly cooked, it will be soft, fluffy, and more than double in volume. If the rice turns out too mushy, cook with a little less water in the next batch. If using a rice cooker, follow the instructions in the manual that came with it.

Glutinous, Sweet, or Sticky Rice *Khao neaw* is a long-grain rice and the main staple in the North and Northeastern regions of Thailand. After it is cooked, it becomes uniquely sticky and soft and can be easily shaped into a ball. Its flavor is mild and sweet. The uncooked grains are whiter, shorter, and rounder than jasmine rice. The best way to prepare glutinous rice is to soak it overnight or for at least three hours in cold water using a ratio of one part rice to three parts water; drain the rice and then steam it over high heat in a Thai bamboo steamer or regular steamer for 15–20 minutes or until tender.

Glutinous Black Rice *Khao neaw dum* is another variety of sweet or sticky rice. It has dark purple grains and a unique fragrance. Prepare it the same way as its white counterpart, but cook it a little longer, about 20–30 minutes overall. Black rice often is combined with glutinous white rice, using a ratio of one to one before soaking, to give it a desirable tender texture after being cooked.

Noodles: *Kuai-tiao* is a Chinese word adopted by Thais to mean noodles or meals with noodles. There are many varieties of noodle, all differing in size, shape, and ingredients. In well-stocked Asian grocery stores in the United States,

Ingredients

you can buy fresh wide or medium rice noodles as well as a fresh sheet that you can slice into noodles at home. Dried noodles are readily available in all sizes and qualities. Dried noodles should be soaked or boiled in water to soften. See photo facing page 32 for various noodles.

Cellophane or Glass Noodles *Woon sen* are made from mung bean flour. They are most often available dried in vermicelli threads. After being soaked or cooked in water, they turn clear (hence the name).

Fine-Thread Rice Noodles *Kanom jeen* are thin, round noodles made from freshly ground rice flour. They are sold in small portions that resemble a bird's nest. *Kanom jeen* is popular for use in many kinds of curry soup. In the United States, fresh noodles are difficult to find. The closest substitute are wheat-based Japanese somen noodles, which are sold in well-stocked Asian grocery stores. Cook the noodles in boiling water until soft. Drain them and rinse with cold water before portioning into small bird's nest-size wads.

Medium Rice Noodles *Kuai-tiao sen lek* are rice noodles that are one-quarter inch wide.

Small Rice Noodles *Kuai-tiao sen mee* are vermicelli rice noodles.

Wide Rice Noodles *Kuai-tiao sen yai* are one-inch-wide rice noodles.

Yellow or Egg Noodles *Bami* are small yellow noodles made from flour and eggs. Fresh noodles are available in well-stocked Asian grocery stores. Dried yellow noodles are also sold prepackaged in small balls. A vegan version of yellow noodles made with an egg substitute is available. Cook the noodles in boiling water until soft.

Mung Beans: *Thua leang* or *thua kiew* are yellow and green respectively and are often used in Thai desserts. The beans are usually sold dried and prepackaged. Soak the beans in cold water for at least two hours before cooking them. Drain and boil the beans in water to cover for 5–7 minutes or until tender.

Thai eggplants

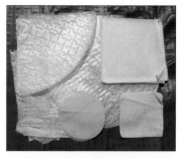

Clockwise from upper left:
Dried rice sheets (triangle and circle)
Frozen lumpia or spring roll wrappers
Fresh wonton wrappers (square)
Fresh pot sticker wrappers (round)
Dried tofu skin or sheets (yellow)

Thai chilies

Fresh wood ear mushrooms

Lemongrass

Galangal

Fresh lesser gingers (kra-chai)

Palm sugar

Bamboo shoots

Top: Large, medium, and small rice noodles
2nd row: Glass (mungbean) noodles and
imitation egg noodles
3rd row: Japanese somen noodles
4th row: Thai kanom jeen rice noodles

Kaffir limes and leaves

Tapioca Pearls: *Saku* are made from tapioca flour and shaped into small, medium, or large round balls. They are kneaded with lukewarm water to make a dough or cooked in boiling water to make pudding.

Wrappers: Thai cooking borrows many Chinese ingredients, especially its wrappers, for a number of dishes. Certain types of ready-made wrappers can be cooked very quickly; this helps speed preparation times instead of making them from scratch. Spring roll wrappers, lumpia wrappers, and rice wrappers are made from a flour-based dough and generally come in three sizes: 5-inch, 9-inch, and 12-inch squares. They are available fresh and frozen. The larger size can be cut according to its use. Wonton wrappers, 3½ inches square, are made from a flour and egg dough and come in two thicknesses: very thin for deep-frying, and thick for steaming or for making dumplings. Tofu sheets or skins also can be used as wrappers. See photo facing page 32 for various wrappers.

Seasonings

Chili Sauce: *Nam jim* is a prepared Thai seasoning that can be used as a condiment or mixed into a dish.

> **Chili Paste with Soybean Oil** *Namprik pow* is a sweet, mild, and smoky chili sauce that often is used as a flavor enhancer in salad dressings and soups.

> **Chinese White Plum Sauce** *Nam jim giem boi* is a mild, sweet-and-sour syrup. It is used as a sauce for delicately flavored dishes such as corn fritters.

> **Sambal Olek** *Namprik dong* is ground, hot-and-sour red chili in a vinegar mixture. It is popular for adding a chili zest to a bowl of soup and various sauces.

> **Sriracha Sauce** *Namprik sriracha* is a hot, sweet-and-sour sauce that can add a spicy heat to any dish.

Fried Spring Rolls, pages 62-63

Ingredients

Sweet Chili Sauce *Nam jim gai* is sweet and sour with evidence of mild red chili chunks. It is a popular sauce for fried or barbecued dishes.

Curry Paste: *Namprik gaeng* comes in many varieties. It is available in small cans for one-time use and in big plastic tubs for several uses. It should always be refrigerated after opening. Ready-made paste is convenient and saves time, but some contain meat products, such as shrimp paste, and preservatives. To all Thai food connoisseurs, a fresh curry paste made from scratch using a mortar and pestle is worth the extra effort.

Maggi Seasoning Sauce: This multipurpose seasoning originated in Switzerland but now is popular throughout Southeast Asia. It serves as a secret flavor enhancer in most marinade recipes. A few drops can improve flavor dramatically. A similar product under the brand name of Golden Mountain Sauce also is available.

Palm or Coconut Sugar: *Nam tan peep* is made from the sap of coconut or palm trees. It has a distinctive flavor and fragrance and a pale, light brown color. In the United States, palm sugar is sold as a paste in glass bottles or as crystallized disks in clear plastic wrap in most well-stocked Asian grocery stores. Chop or grate it into small chunks, or heat in a microwave for 2–3 minutes to melt, to measure it before using. Store the same way as ordinary sugar. See photo, facing page 32.

Soy Sauces: See Soy Products, page 13.

Stir-fry Sauce: *Nam mun hed* is similar to oyster sauce but is made from plant-based ingredients, such as mushrooms with sweetened soy sauce, and is used mostly in vegetable stir-fry dishes. It comes in many varieties: mushroom stir-fry sauce, vegetarian stir-fry sauce, and vegetarian marinade sauce. It must be refrigerated after opening and should last about six months.

Vegetable Base or Bouillon: *Prung ros* is a flavor enhancer made by reducing vegetable stock into a paste or powder. It adds sodium and an intense vegetable flavor. It is used sparingly to improve the taste of a dish without using MSG.

Special Equipment

Mortar and Pestle: There are two types of mortars and pestles, each serving a particular purpose: *krok hin*, a stone mortar, and *krok din*, a clay mortar. The *krok hin* mortar (bowl) and *saak* (pestle) are made of solid granite or sandstone and are hand carved from a selected piece of the stone by krok artisans. The mortar is very heavy and sturdy and has a stubby shape; its mouth is wide and has a very thick rim. It's perfect for the heavy pounding required for making chili and curry pastes.

Krok din is easy to make by hand. The mortar is made of clay and kiln fired, and its pestle is carved out of wood. It is a lot less expensive than the *krok hin*, but it has a shorter life and is disposable. It is shaped like a tall cylinder, with a wide mouth and a narrow base. It is light, unstable, and not suitable for making pastes. Its main function is to serve as a mixing or tossing bowl, with little grinding. The famous Green Papaya Salad *Som Tum*, page 57, uses this kind of mortar to mix and toss its ingredients.

Steamer: Thai people invented a cylindrical bamboo steamer to cook the sweet, sticky, long-grain rice, which is called by various names in the United States: sweet rice, sticky rice, or glutinous rice, as in the dessert Sticky Rice and Mangoes, page 168. A bamboo steamer set comes with a bamboo cylinder and a narrow-neck pot for boiling water. The bamboo cylinder is hand woven from dried bamboo strips into a cone shape, about ten inches in diameter at the opening and about twelve inches tall. The cylinder will sit tightly fitted on a narrow-neck pot of boiling water. Any kind of lid that fits in the cylinder can be used to trap the steam. A regular steamer or Chinese bamboo steamer (the type of steamer used for dim sum) could also be used by lining its steam tray with cheesecloth so the rice grains won't fall through the steaming holes.

Wok: The Thai people borrowed wok and stir-fry cooking techniques from the Chinese and now the wok has become indispensable in the Thai kitchen. This thin metal bowl with handle is serves many purposes: stir-frying, deep-frying, steaming, boiling, smoking, and more. It traditionally is made of rolled steel, which provides excellent heat control, but it also can be made of sheet iron, anodized aluminum, or stainless steel. It comes in various sizes—from small, with one long handle for tossing food, to large, with two handles to manage a large volume of food. The advantage of wok cooking and stir-frying, especially for a mixture that includes a lot of vegetables, lies in its speed, which consequently minimizes the loss of vitamins, color, and flavor in fresh food. A flat-bottom wok has been introduced for use on an electric stove or a flat-top range in the Western kitchen. Good maintenance is required to season the wok after each use so it won't rust. Clean and dry the wok thoroughly; then heat it and rub it all over with a little vegetable oil.

Buddha's
Table

Curry Pastes and Sauces

Any complete Thai meal includes a curry dish or chili dip or both. A mortar and pestle are used in every Thai kitchen for grinding. These days, for convenience and to save time, ready-made curry pastes are available in many varieties and are sold in small cans or jars and in large plastic tubs. They should be refrigerated after opening. But to all Thai food connoisseurs, a fresh curry paste made from scratch with a mortar and pestle is worth the trouble.

Thai people use the *krok* (mortar) and *saak* (pestle) almost daily to grind and mix herbs and spices to make various pastes for their meals. In this part of the world, we would probably switch to a high-tech blender or food processor. However, most Thai chefs will attest that a mortar and pestle produces far better chili and curry pastes because the grinding and pounding motion breaks down the essences and oils in the ingredients better. A good mortar and pestle, along with secret recipes for curry pastes, are handed down from mother to daughter through many generations and are considered family heirlooms.

Thai curries have much Indian influence with such spices as cumin and coriander. But Thais have added a number of local spices, including fresh and dried chilies, to create a variety of curries to call their own. The process of making a paste is not complicated, but it is long and monotonous. It takes twenty to thirty minutes to grind ingredients into a smooth paste. Principal ingredients are garlic, shallots, chilies, lemongrass, galangal, kaffir lime, Indian spices, and a knockout, pungent flavor enhancer, fermented bean curds. The colors of the chilies used determine the kind of curry and the heat intensity of the dish, such as the

39

hot and sweet Green Curry, page 139, the pungent Red Curry, page 143, and the aromatic and mild Panaeng Curry, page 146, and Yellow Curry, page 147.

Many well-established Thai restaurants prepare their own fresh chili and curry pastes. Their recipes vary from one place to another in the amount and proportion of each ingredient used to create a well-balanced flavor. A good fresh paste makes a world of difference in a curry soup. The most famous Thai curry dishes in the United States are Green Curry *Gaeng Keow Wan*, page 139, and Panaeng Curry *Gaeng Panaeng*, page 146. It is such a satisfying, indulgent experience to have a smoldering, aromatic curry soup with hot steamed rice. Both dishes use coconut milk for a creamy base. But don't despair if you're not a coconut lover. Many Thai chili and curry dishes are prepared without coconut, such as Tofu Patties *Tod Mun*, page 82, Red Curry Green Beans *Pad Prik King*, page 111, Hunter Soup *Gaeng Paa*, page 94, or Sour Curry Soup *Gaeng Som*, page 97. For your convenience, all curry pastes come prepackaged and ready to use. While packaged pastes are handy, there is no way to control their heat intensity, which often is inconsistent. In addition, preservatives may be added. That's why I prefer to make my own fresh pastes, and you might, too. You also can modify a recipe to suit your taste.

Chili Dipping Sauce

Makes 1 cup

This is a multipurpose sauce that is easy to make and has a usual spot on the Thai dining table. It helps add extra tastes of salty, sour, sweet, and spicy to any dish. It also can be a sauce for a number of fried or barbecued dishes. During a hard time, a Thai could survive for months on this minimal provision, eating this sauce over rice and vegetables.

3 tablespoons light soy sauce

3 tablespoons fresh lime juice

1 tablespoon sugar, more or less to taste

1 tablespoon chopped fresh Thai chilies, more or less to taste

1 tablespoon thinly sliced garlic

1 tablespoon thinly sliced shallots

1 tablespoon chopped fresh cilantro leaves

1 tablespoon chopped green onions

Combine all the ingredients and stir to mix well.

Chili Sweet Soy

Makes I cup

This is a more elaborate multipurpose sauce that goes well with grilled or fried dishes, such as grilled mushrooms and eggplants, corn fritters, or fried sweet potatoes. Its flavor is more complex with domineering sweet and sublime ginger. Its chili heat can be easily adjusted by the amount of red chili sauce added. This sauce can be prepared in a large batch and stored in the refrigerator. It should keep about two weeks.

$^1/2$ cup soy sauce

$^3/4$ cup packed brown sugar

3 tablespoons finely diced onions

2 tablespoons tomato paste

2 tablespoons rice vinegar or distilled white vinegar

2 tablespoons finely diced fresh ginger

I tablespoon red chili sauce [*sambal olek*] or Tabasco, more or less to taste

Combine the soy sauce and sugar in a small saucepan. Place over medium heat and cook for 7–10 minutes or until the sugar is dissolved and the mixture thickens. Remove from the heat and let cool. Stir in the onions, tomato paste, vinegar, ginger, and red chili sauce. Serve on the side with grilled and satay dishes.

Gaeng Koa Curry Paste

Makes 1 cup

Gaeng koa is a simple version of Thai red curry paste that has less complex flavors and less spicy ingredients than other curries. Its simplicity allows the flavor of the food it's cooked with to shine.

Stem and seed the dried chilies. Soak them in warm water for 10–15 minutes or until soft. Drain and squeeze dry.

Using a mortar and pestle, pound and grind all the ingredients, adding in each new ingredient only after the previous one is puréed and incorporated into a paste. Continue pounding and grinding until the mixture forms a smooth paste. Alternatively, combine all of the ingredients in a food processor and process into a smooth paste, adding a small amount of water to facilitate blending.

6–8 large dried red chilies (California, New Mexico, or guajillo chilies)

1 tablespoon chopped fresh red Thai chilies (optional, for more heat)

3 tablespoons chopped shallots

2 tablespoons chopped lemongrass, tender midsection only

2 tablespoons chopped garlic

1 tablespoon chopped galangal

1 tablespoon chopped fresh cilantro roots or stems

1 teaspoon chopped kaffir lime skin or leaves

1 teaspoon whole black peppercorns

1 teaspoon salt

1 teaspoon fermented bean curds (optional)

Green Curry Paste

Homemade green curry paste is the freshest curry of all. To obtain the green color, fresh green chilies are used, in contrast with the dried chilies in the red and yellow curry pastes. All the fresh ingredients produce refreshing flavors that make green the most popular Thai curry. Fresh cilantro leaves can be processed and added to the paste for a more intense green color.

Roast the coriander, cumin, and peppercorns in a dry pan over medium heat for 3–5 minutes or until fragrant.

Using a mortar and pestle, pound and grind all the ingredients, adding in each new ingredient only after the previous one is puréed and incorporated into a paste. Continue pounding and grinding until the mixture forms a smooth paste. Alternatively, combine all of the ingredients in a food processor and process into a smooth paste, adding a small amount of water to facilitate blending.

Namprik Gaeng Keow Wan

I tablespoon whole coriander seeds

2 teaspoons whole cumin seeds

I teaspoon whole black peppercorns

10 fresh green Thai chilies, chopped

5 large fresh green chilies (serrano or jalapeño), chopped

3 tablespoons chopped lemongrass, tender midsection only

3 tablespoons chopped shallots

2 tablespoons chopped garlic

2 tablespoons chopped fresh cilantro roots or stems

I tablespoon chopped galangal

2 teaspoons fermented bean curds (optional)

I teaspoon chopped kaffir lime skin or leaves

I teaspoon salt

Hunter Curry Paste

Makes 1 cup

Gaeng paa *curry paste is also a simple red curry that goes well with clear broth as a base instead of coconut milk. Its simplicity is derived from ingredients that hunters can gather in the woods or make from a small container of provisions. The curry paste flavors the broth and the mixture becomes a curry dish that is considered a soup.*

6–8 large dried red chilies (California, New Mexico, or guajillo chilies)

2 teaspoons whole coriander seeds

1 teaspoon whole black peppercorns

3 tablespoons chopped lemongrass, tender midsection only

3 tablespoons chopped shallots

2 tablespoons chopped garlic

2 tablespoons chopped galangal

1 tablespoon chopped kaffir lime skin or leaves

1 tablespoon chopped fresh red Thai chilies (optional, for more heat)

1 teaspoon salt

1 teaspoon fermented bean curds (optional)

Stem and seed the dried chilies. Soak them in warm water for 10–15 minutes or until soft. Drain and squeeze dry.

Roast the coriander seeds and peppercorns in a dry pan over medium heat for 3–5 minutes or until fragrant. Let cool.

Using a mortar and pestle, pound and grind all the ingredients, adding in each new ingredient only after the previous one is puréed and incorporated into a paste. Continue pounding and grinding until the mixture forms a smooth paste. Alternatively, combine all of the ingredients in a food processor and process into a smooth paste, adding a small amount of water to facilitate blending.

Massamun Curry Paste

Makes 1 cup

Massamun is the heartiest of all Thai stew-like curries. This curry paste is complex and elaborate, containing more ingredients, especially dried-roasted flavors, than any other curry pastes. Many Thai chefs have a version of this recipe, using their own secrets and intensities. After you do your own research and trials, adjust the ingredients to fit your taste—this will make the best massamun curry.

6–8 large dried red chilies (California, New Mexico, or guajillo chilies)

2 tablespoons whole coriander seeds

2 teaspoons whole cumin seeds

5 whole cardamom seeds

1 small cinnamon stick

1 whole nutmeg

5 whole cloves

1 teaspoon whole black peppercorns

3 tablespoons chopped shallots

2 tablespoons chopped lemongrass, tender midsection only

2 tablespoons chopped garlic

1 tablespoon chopped galangal

1 tablespoon chopped fresh cilantro roots or stems

2 teaspoons chopped kaffir lime skin or leaves

2 teaspoons fermented bean curds (optional)

1 teaspoon salt

Stem and seed the dried red chilies. Soak them in warm water for 10–15 minutes or until soft. Drain and squeeze dry.

Roast the coriander, cumin, cardamom, cinnamon, nutmeg, cloves, and peppercorns in a dry pan over medium heat for 5–7 minutes or until fragrant.

Using a mortar and pestle, pound and grind all the ingredients, adding in each new ingredient only after the previous one is puréed and incorporated into a paste. Continue pounding and grinding until the mixture forms a smooth paste. Alternatively, combine all of the ingredients in a food processor and process into a smooth paste, adding a small amount of water to facilitate blending.

Panaeng Curry Paste

Makes 1 cup

Malaysian influence gives this curry a unique flavor, due mainly to the addition of roasted peanuts to the curry paste. Panaeng curry usually is drier than most Thai curries. Its dryness is achieved by reduction, which, at the end, leaves the curry with an intense taste.

Stem and seed the dried red chilies. Soak them in warm water for 10–15 minutes or until soft. Drain and squeeze dry.

Roast the coriander and cumin seeds in a dry pan over medium heat for 3–5 minutes or until fragrant.

Using a mortar and pestle, pound and grind all the ingredients, adding in each new ingredient only after the previous one is puréed and incorporated into a paste. Continue pounding and grinding until the mixture forms a smooth paste. Alternatively, combine all of the ingredients in a food processor and process into a smooth paste, adding a small amount of water to facilitate blending.

Namprik Panaeng

6–8 large dried red chilies (New Mexico, California, or guajillo chilies)

1 tablespoon whole coriander seeds

2 teaspoons whole cumin seeds

3 tablespoons chopped roasted peanuts

2 tablespoons chopped lemongrass, tender midsection only

2 tablespoons chopped shallots

2 tablespoons chopped garlic

1 tablespoon chopped fresh red Thai chilies (optional, for more heat)

1 tablespoon chopped galangal

1 tablespoon chopped kaffir lime skin or leaves

1 tablespoon chopped fresh cilantro roots or stems

2 teaspoons fermented bean curds (optional)

1 teaspoon salt

Peanut Sauce

Makes 2 cups

Satay, grilled food on skewers, is not complete without peanut sauce. Thai cuisine has modified the original recipe from Indonesia, creating the sweetest and creamiest peanut sauce of all. Spicy, rich, and creamy sauce often is accompanied by cold, refreshing Cucumber Salad Ajad, page 67, as a palate cleanser. If this recipe is too rich for your taste, try Peanut Sauce #2, page 49, which is simpler and closer to the original version.

Nam Jeem Satay

2 ½ cups coconut cream

⅓ cup Red Curry Paste, page 50, or 3 tablespoons ready-made paste

¾ cup ground peanuts or chunky peanut butter

¼ cup grated palm sugar, or more to taste

3 tablespoons light soy sauce or soy paste, or more to taste

2 tablespoons tamarind liquid, or 1 tablespoon rice vinegar

1 tablespoon vegetable base, or 1 vegetable bouillon cube

Salt

Combine ½ cup of the coconut cream and Red Curry Paste in a medium saucepan over medium heat. Cook 3–5 minutes or until fragrant.

Add the remaining coconut cream, ground peanuts, sugar, soy sauce, tamarind liquid, and vegetable base. Cook, stirring constantly, for 5–7 minutes or until the ground peanuts are completely dissolved and all ingredients are well combined. Make sure the ground peanuts do not burn on the bottom of the pan. Season with salt to taste and adjust any other seasonings, if necessary. Serve the sauce on the side with satay dishes.

Peanut Sauce #2

Makes 1 ½ cups

Using a mortar and pestle, crush the garlic and chilies until well blended. Add the peanuts and grind to incorporate well. Add the sweet soy sauce and fresh lime juice and work the pestle until the mixture is well combined. Season with salt to taste and adjust any other seasonings, if necessary. Add a little water if the sauce is too thick. Alternately, place all of the ingredients in a food processor and process until well combined, adding a small amount of water to facilitate blending.

2 tablespoons minced garlic

2 fresh Thai chilies, more or less to taste

⅓ cup roasted peanuts or peanut paste, or more to taste

¼ cup Indonesian sweet soy sauce [*ketjap manis*], or more to taste

¼ cup fresh lime juice, or more to taste

Salt

Red Curry Paste

Makes 1 cup

Red curry or gaeng ped curry paste is the most versatile and all kinds of ingredients can be incorporated with the paste to make a variety of soups, salads, curries, and stir-fries. Extra spices, usually nutmeg, caraway, or kra-chai (lesser ginger), can be added to enhance the flavor of the food it is cooked with. Red curry paste can be personalized by adding or subtracting ingredients to fit your individual taste.

6–8 large dried red chilies (New Mexico, California, or guajillo chilies)

1 tablespoon whole coriander seeds

2 teaspoons whole cumin seeds

3 tablespoons chopped shallots

3 tablespoons chopped fresh cilantro roots or stems

2 tablespoons chopped lemongrass, tender midsection only

2 tablespoons chopped fresh red Thai chilies (optional, for more heat)

2 tablespoons chopped garlic

1 tablespoon chopped galangal

1 tablespoon chopped kaffir lime skin or leaves

2 teaspoons fermented bean curds (optional)

1 teaspoon salt

Stem and seed the dried chilies. Soak them in warm water for 10–15 minutes or until soft. Drain and squeeze dry.

Roast the cumin and coriander seeds in a dry pan over medium heat for 3–5 minutes or until fragrant.

Using a mortar and pestle, pound and grind all the ingredients, adding in each new ingredient only after the previous one is puréed and incorporated into a paste. Continue pounding and grinding until the mixture forms a smooth paste. Alternatively, combine all of the ingredients in a food processor and process into a smooth paste, adding a small amount of water to facilitate blending.

Sour Curry Paste

Makes 1 cup

Sour curry paste is another version of red curry used to make a clear broth, which is considered a curry soup. It uses Thai lesser ginger [kra-chai] as a main herb that imparts a distinctive flavor to this curry. Sour curry, as the name implies, has a leading sour taste derived from tamarind, a local Thai product, which is valued for its unique sweet-and-sour flavor.

6 large dried red chilies (New Mexico, California, or guajillo chilies)

1/4 cup chopped lesser ginger [*kra-chai*]

3 tablespoons chopped shallots

2 tablespoons chopped lemongrass, tender midsection only

2 tablespoons chopped garlic

1 tablespoon chopped fresh red Thai chilies (optional, for more heat)

1 tablespoon chopped galangal

1 tablespoon chopped kaffir lime skin or leaves

2 teaspoons fermented bean curds (optional)

1 teaspoon salt

Stem and seed the dried chilies. Soak them in warm water for 10–15 minutes or until soft. Drain and squeeze dry.

Using a mortar and pestle, pound and grind all the ingredients, adding in each new ingredient only after the previous one is puréed and incorporated into a paste. Continue pounding and grinding until the mixture forms a smooth paste. Alternatively, combine all of the ingredients in a food processor and process into a smooth paste, adding a small amount of water to facilitate blending.

Yellow Curry Paste

Makes 3/4 cup

Namprik Gaeng Garee

This curry paste is a direct descendant of Indian curry, with the small modification of added lemongrass and kaffir lime for the Thai palate. The word "garee" is derived from the Indian "curry" powder, whose yellow color obviously carries the name.

6 large dried red chilies (California, New Mexico, or guajillo chilies)

2 teaspoons whole coriander seeds

1 teaspoon whole cumin seeds

3 tablespoons chopped lemongrass, tender midsection only

2 tablespoons curry powder

2 tablespoons chopped shallots

2 tablespoons chopped garlic

1 tablespoon chopped galangal

1 tablespoon chopped fresh ginger

2 teaspoons chopped kaffir lime skin or leaves

1 teaspoon salt

Stem and seed the dried chilies. Soak them in warm water for 10–15 minutes or until soft. Drain and squeeze dry.

Roast the coriander and cumin seeds in a dry pan over medium heat for 3–5 minutes or until fragrant.

Using a mortar and pestle, pound and grind all the ingredients, adding in each new ingredient only after the previous one is puréed and incorporated into a paste. Continue pounding and grinding until the mixture forms a smooth paste. Alternatively, combine all of the ingredients in a food processor and process into a smooth paste, adding a small amount of water to facilitate blending.

Salads, Snacks, and Appetizers

Thai Salads

Thai salad [*yum*] can be a main dish when accompanied with plenty of vegetables on the side, or it can be served with plain rice as one of many dishes in a meal. Thai salads are easy to make: simply toss together fresh and cooked ingredients and add a dressing or seasonings, usually lime juice (sour), light soy sauce (salt), and sugar (sweet). Thai salads are characterized as having refreshing and intense flavors. Lime juice mixes harmoniously with the soy sauce and sugar and imparts a clean, sharp taste. Oil is used in Thai salads only for cooking those ingredients that require a crunchy texture, such as fried sliced garlic or shallots for garnishes. Other ingredients that must be cooked prior to being added to the salad, such as potatoes or eggplants, are best either poached or grilled.

Not only is the right combination of sour, salt, and sweet tastes critical for a Thai salad, the right texture also is important. Some ingredients must be prepared in advance before they can be tossed with the dressing. These range in texture from soft, gluey, and firm, to hard and crunchy (with the crunch coming mostly from roasted peanuts). Different ingredients and textures are used as garnishes to tie together all the flavors and produce a well-balanced salad. Chopped cilantro and green onions make a pleasing garnish to top most Thai salads. Fresh or crunchy fried chilies add an element of surprise, as the heat of the chilies will explode in the mouth.

Banana Flower Salad

Serves 6

This is a salad for those looking for new and exciting flavors and textures. Banana flower is the male part at the tip of a banana red inflorescence. It first needs to be de-bittered by boiling in water and then thinly sliced for this salad. If banana flowers are impossible to find, unripe green bananas or plantains can be used. Peel the bananas and cook them the same way as the flowers.

2 whole banana flowers

1 cup julienne fried or firm tofu

3 tablespoons thinly sliced shallots

3 tablespoons fresh lime juice, or more to taste

2 tablespoons coconut cream (optional)

2 tablespoons light soy sauce, or more to taste

2 tablespoons chili paste with soybean oil
[*nam prik pow*]

1 tablespoon sugar, or more to taste

1 tablespoon chopped fresh Thai chilies,
more or less to taste

1 head of lettuce, cleaned and cut into bite-size pieces

2 tablespoons chopped fresh cilantro leaves, for garnish

2 tablespoons chopped green onions, for garnish

Cut the banana flowers in half lengthwise. Strip and discard their red outer sheaths until you reach the light pink and white inner parts. Trim off the stems.

Place 6 cups of water in a medium saucepan and bring to a boil. Add the flowers and simmer for 7–10 minutes or until tender. Drain and cut the flowers crosswise into thin strips to make 2–3 cups.

Combine the banana flowers, tofu, shallots, lime juice, optional coconut cream, soy sauce, chili paste with soybean oil, sugar, and Thai chilies in a large bowl. Gently toss to mix well. Adjust the flavor by adding more soy sauce, sugar, and lime juice to taste.

Line a serving platter with a bed of the lettuce. Top with the salad and garnish with the chopped cilantro and green onions.

Corn Fritters

Serves 6

Sweet crunchiness makes this dish highly appealing. In the United States, sweet corn in season makes the best staple for this simple dish. The best corn, combined with exotic ingredients, is the recipe for delicious success.

4 ears fresh corn, kernels cut from the cobs (about 2 cups)

3 tablespoons all-purpose flour, or more as needed

2 tablespoons cornstarch

2 tablespoons finely minced shallots

2 tablespoons finely minced garlic

2 tablespoons finely minced fresh ginger

2 tablespoons minced green onions, green part only

1 tablespoon ground coriander

2 teaspoons baking soda

1 teaspoon chili powder or paprika (optional)

1 teaspoon salt

1/4 cup crumbled silken tofu, or a little water, to bind

4 cups peanut oil or vegetable oil for frying

Combine the corn kernels, flour, cornstarch, shallots, garlic, ginger, green onions, coriander, baking soda, optional chili powder, and salt in a large bowl and mix well. Add the silken tofu or water a little at a time to help bind the mixture. The texture should be stiff, like cookie dough, and hold together to make patties. Be careful not to add too much liquid.

Place the oil in a deep frying pan or wok and heat to 375°F. The oil should have a depth of at least two inches. With damp hands, form 1 tablespoon of batter into a flat, round patty. Drop it into the hot oil and lightly aerate the batter by jabbing it with a fork. Repeat the process until the fritters loosely fill the pan. Cook for 2–3 minutes on each side until golden brown all over.

Remove the fritters from the oil with a slotted spoon and drain on absorbent paper or paper towels. Serve the corn fritters with Chili Sweet Soy, page 42, or Cucumber Salad *Ajad*, page 67, or ready-made Thai sweet chili sauce.

Creamy Green Bean Salad

Serves 6

Yum Thaou

Thai salads are mostly light with simple dressings of lime juice, seasonings, and herbs, without any oil. This salad is an exception, as coconut cream is used in its rich, sweet, creamy dressing. The Thai ready-made condiment namprik pow (chili paste with soybean oil), which is made with roasted chilies, provides an essence of smoky aroma to this complex dish.

- 3 large dried red chilies, stemmed and seeded (California or New Mexico chilies)
- 2 tablespoons chopped shallots
- I tablespoon chopped garlic
- I teaspoon salt
- 3 tablespoons sweetened coconut flakes or shredded coconut
- 2 cups green beans or long beans, thinly sliced crosswise
- I cup julienne fried or firm tofu
- 2 tablespoons coconut cream
- 2 tablespoons light soy sauce, or more to taste
- 2 tablespoons fresh lime juice, or more to taste
- 2 tablespoons chili paste with soybean oil [*namprik pow*]
- I tablespoon sugar, or more to taste
- I head of lettuce, cleaned and cut into bite-size pieces
- 2 tablespoons chopped fresh cilantro leaves, for garnish
- 2 tablespoons chopped green onions, for garnish

Roast the chilies, shallots, and garlic in a dry pan over medium heat for 5–7 minutes or until fragrant. Using a mortar and pestle or a food processor, process the roasted ingredients until finely ground. Stir in the salt and set aside.

Roast the coconut flakes in a dry pan over medium heat for 7–10 minutes or until light brown and fragrant. Remove from the pan and set aside.

Place 3 cups of water in a saucepan and bring to a boil. Add the green beans and blanch them for 2 minutes. Drain and immediately plunge them into a bowl of cold water. Drain and pat dry.

Transfer the beans to a large bowl and add the tofu, chili mixture, coconut cream, soy sauce, lime juice, chili paste with soybean oil, and sugar. Toss well. Add the roasted coconut flakes and toss again. Adjust the flavor by adding more soy sauce, sugar, and lime juice to taste.

Line a serving platter with a bed of the lettuce. Top with the green bean mixture and garnish with the cilantro and green onions.

Green Papaya Salad

Serves 6

Papayas grow abundantly in the tropical climate of Thailand. Their seeds are spread mostly by birds. The hearty papaya tree could grow well on only a narrow strip of soil, such as a plot between a house and a fence. Most Thai households have at least one papaya tree, whose unripe green fruits could be harvested easily for this salad. In the United States, the green papaya is hard to find; cucumber, green beans, or long beans may be used as substitutes. Thai people use a clay mortar and pestle to mix and fold all the ingredients to ensure that the seasonings permeate the dense texture of the papaya, carrots, and long beans. If the mortar and pestle are not available, use a steel bowl with a rolling pin to grind and mix the salad. Do not use a food processor; its blade will cut the ingredients too fine, causing them to lose their crunchy texture and resulting in too much liquid.

2 cups peeled and shredded firm, fresh green papaya (1 1/2–2 pounds papaya)
1 cup shredded carrots
1 cup shredded jicama (optional)
1 tablespoon chopped garlic
1 tablespoon minced fresh Thai chilies, more or less to taste
1/2 cup sliced long beans, in 2-inch lengths
1/2 cup coarsely chopped tomatoes
1/4 cup chopped roasted peanuts
1/4 cup fresh lime juice, or more to taste
1/4 cup light soy sauce, or more to taste
2 tablespoons finely minced or melted palm sugar, or more to taste
1 head cabbage or lettuce, cleaned and cut into bite-site pieces

(See photo, facing page 128.)

Select a firm green papaya. Peel the papaya completely and use only the white meat. Rinse with cold water and shred into fine matchsticks with a shredder or mandolin. Peel the carrot and optional jicama and shred into fine matchsticks.

Crush the garlic in a clay mortar with pestle or a bowl with a rolling pin. Add and crush the chilies, then add the long beans and continue crushing until well mixed. Add the papaya, carrot, and jicama. Lightly pound the pestle while simultaneously using a large spoon to toss the mixture. Continue pounding and tossing until well combined. Add the tomatoes, peanuts, lime juice, soy sauce, and sugar. Continue pounding and tossing to mix well and evenly distribute the flavors.

Taste the salad and adjust the flavor with more soy sauce, lime juice, and sugar to taste. Serve with the cabbage or lettuce on the side.

Crêpes

Serves 6

French influences came from afar and spread across Southeast Asia. The word "yuan" suggests Vietnamese cuisine from the French origin, whose comparable dish can be found in high-end Vietnamese restaurants. Thais have adapted the dish, modified the taste, and added ingredients, such as shredded coconut, to call it their own. The dish requires many steps of preparation and many elaborate ingredients that were originally fit for the royal court. You can also find this dish at a specialized hawker's stand. Special occasions call for a special feast and Kanom Bueng Yuan *is a worthy contender.*

BATTER:

3/4 cup rice flour

1/2 cup coconut milk

1/2 cup water, or more as needed

1/4 cup all-purpose flour

1 whole egg (optional)

2 tablespoons vegetable oil

1 tablespoon sugar

2 teaspoons turmeric

1 teaspoon baking soda

1/2 teaspoon salt

Combine all the batter ingredients in a bowl and gently beat until smooth. Set aside to rest for 30 minutes. Before using, dilute with a little more water if the batter is too thick. The texture should be like a thin pancake batter.

Preheat the oven to 350°F. Place the shredded coconut in a baking pan and roast it in the oven until lightly browned. Alternatively, roast the coconut in a dry skillet over medium heat for 5–7 minutes or until light brown and fragrant. Remove from the pan and set aside.

Heat a large saucepan over medium heat, add the oil, and sauté the garlic and shallots for 2–3 minutes or until fragrant. Add the tofu and mushrooms and sauté until the mushrooms are tender, about 3 minutes. Add the peanuts, optional turnips, soy sauce, sugar, pepper, and roasted shredded coconut. Stir to mix well. Add a little water if the mixture seems too dry. Remove from the heat and set aside.

Place a 10-inch nonstick skillet over medium heat and brush it with just enough oil to coat the surface. Pour about ⅓ cup of the batter into the pan and swirl the batter to thinly coat the pan's surface. Pour off any excess batter so the crêpe can be very thin. Cook the batter for 2–5 minutes or until firm and the surface is dry. Do not attempt to turn over the crêpe.

Add about ¾ cup of the filling, spreading it over half of the crêpe. Top the filling with ⅓ cup of the bean sprouts and 1 tablespoon of the cilantro. Fold over the other half of the crêpe to cover the filling.

FILLING:

¾ cup sweetened shredded coconut or coconut flakes

2 tablespoons vegetable oil, or more as needed

2 tablespoons minced garlic

2 tablespoons minced shallots

2 cups julienne fried or firm tofu

2 cups coarsely chopped mushrooms of your choice

½ cup chopped roasted peanuts

¼ cup minced preserved turnips (optional)

3 tablespoons light soy sauce

2 tablespoons sugar

½ teaspoon pepper

2 cups bean sprouts, more for garnish

½ cup chopped fresh cilantro leaves, for garnish

½ cup julienne colored bell peppers (red, orange, or yellow), for garnish

To remove the crêpe from the pan, invert a serving plate and cover the top of the pan. Place your hand over the plate and turn over the pan to flip the crêpe onto the plate. Repeat the process until all of the batter and filling have been used, making about 6 large crêpes or more small ones by reducing the size of the crêpes.

Garnish each crêpe with more cilantro and some of the bell pepper slices. Serve with Cucumber Salad *Ajad*, page 67.

Crispy Noodles

Serves 6

Only experienced cooks, through trial and error, can perfect this rather complicated dish. Practice and perseverance will help bring about a delicious result. My mother, whose noodles stayed crispy longer than anybody else's, was well known for her mee grop. Unfortunately, her secret recipe died with her and I still cannot replicate her specialty. This dish requires many steps and ingredients to prepare. The noodles are fried until they are crisp and lightly puffed with air. Then they are tossed with a sweet-and-sour sauce. It is great as an appetizer; you won't be able to stop after the first bite.

NOODLES:

4 cups vegetable oil for deep-frying

4 ounces dried vermicelli rice noodles [*sen mee*]

1/4 cup very thinly sliced shallots, for garnish

CRISPY NOODLES SAUCE:

2 tablespoons vegetable oil

2 tablespoons minced shallots

2 tablespoons minced garlic

3/4 cup rice vinegar or distilled white vinegar

3/4 cup palm sugar, grated or melted

1/2 cup sugar

1/2 cup light soy sauce

3 tablespoons tomato paste (for red coloring)

2 tablespoons fresh lime juice

1 tablespoon vegetable base, or 1 vegetable bouillon cube

Place the oil in a wok or large pan and heat it to 400°F. Make sure that the oil is very hot before deep-frying the noodles. Separate the noodles into four equal portions. Drop one portion at a time into the hot oil and fry until fully puffed, about 3 seconds on each side, turning the noodles once with a large wire strainer or slotted spoon. Remove from the oil with a slotted spoon and drain on absorbent paper or paper towels. The crunchy fried noodles can be kept overnight if wrapped and sealed tightly.

Fry the shallots in the hot oil for 2–3 minutes or until light brown and crispy; do not burn. Remove from the oil with a slotted spoon and drain on absorbent paper or paper towels. Set aside for garnish.

To make the sauce, place the oil in a medium saucepan over medium-low heat. Add the shallots and garlic and sauté 2–3 minutes or until fragrant. Stir in the remaining sauce ingredients and simmer 20–30 minutes or until the mixture is thick and syrupy. The sauce must be thick enough to coat the back of a spoon and cling to the noodles. Watery sauce will moisten and soften the noodles and destroy their crisp texture. The sauce needs to be warm and fluid for ease of mixing. If necessary, warm the sauce over low heat before combining with the noodles.

Heat a small amount of vegetable oil in a skillet. Add the tofu and mushrooms and sauté over medium heat until the mushrooms are tender, about 5 minutes. Stir in a little of the prepared Crispy Noodles Sauce, just enough to coat the mixture. Set aside.

GARNISHES:

2 cups julienne fried or firm tofu

2 cups coarsely chopped wood ear mushrooms or other mushrooms of your choice

$1/4$ cup sliced garlic chives or green onions, in 1-inch lengths

$1/4$ cup julienne red bell peppers

3 tablespoons chopped fresh cilantro leaves

2 tablespoons thinly sliced pickled garlic or fresh garlic

2 tablespoons orange zest

2 cups fresh bean sprouts

Just before serving, transfer the noodles to a large bowl. Gently fold in the tofu and mushrooms. Sprinkle with the sauce, adding a little at a time, and gently fold it in so the sauce evenly coats the noodles. Taste the mixture and add more sauce if needed.

Transfer to a serving platter and sprinkle with the fried shallots, chives, red bell peppers, chopped cilantro, pickled garlic, and orange zest. Arrange the fresh bean sprouts next to the noodles on the platter before serving.

Fried Spring Rolls

Serves 6

The Chinese influence over Southeast Asia is so great that each country has developed its own kind of spring roll, created its own name for it, and embellished it with its own local flavors. The Thai version is served with a spicy dipping sauce or any spicy bottled condiment. Ready-made spring roll wrappers are widely available fresh (look in the refrigerated section) or frozen in most grocery stores. Many brands of wrappers contain egg products, so read the ingredients panel carefully if you wish to avoid eggs. Rice paper wrappers and fresh or dried tofu sheets or skins are also readily available. In addition to frying, the tofu sheet wrappers are suitable for steaming. (See photo, facing page 33.)

SPRING ROLLS:

2 ounces dried vermicelli rice noodles [*sen mee*] or glass noodles [*woon sen*]

2 cups julienne mushrooms of your choice

1 cup julienne firm tofu

1 cup julienne celery

3 tablespoons minced fresh cilantro roots or stems

3 tablespoons minced garlic

2 tablespoons sugar

2 tablespoons light soy sauce

2 tablespoons Maggi Seasoning Sauce

1 tablespoon vegetable base, or 1 vegetable bouillon cube, finely crumbled

1 teaspoon pepper

1/2 teaspoon salt

1 package spring roll, lumpia, or tofu sheet wrappers (5 1/2–6 inches square)

1 cup bean sprouts (optional)

4 cups vegetable oil for deep-frying

Soak the noodles in warm water until soft, about 30 minutes; refresh with several changes of water if necessary. Drain and cut into 4-inch lengths.

To make the stuffing, combine the mushrooms, tofu, celery, cilantro, garlic, sugar, soy sauce, Maggi Seasoning Sauce, vegetable base, pepper, and salt in a large bowl. Mix until well combined.

Place about 2 tablespoons of the stuffing at one end of each wrapper, and form it into a 3-inch-long log. Arrange the noodles and optional bean sprouts horizontally over the log. Roll up the wrapper tightly halfway and then fold in both ends. Continue wrapping and then apply some water on the open edges before sealing completely.

Pour the oil in a deep pan and heat to 375°F. The oil should have a depth of at least two inches. Lower the spring rolls into the pan to fit loosely. Fry the spring rolls, turning occasionally, for 5–7 minutes or until golden brown and crispy on all sides. Remove from the oil and drain on absorbent paper or paper towels.

Serve the spring rolls whole or cut in half, with dipping sauce (recipe follows), ready-made Thai sweet chili sauce, or sriracha sauce on the side.

To make the dipping sauce, combine all the ingredients in a small bowl and stir until the sugar is dissolved.

DIPPING SAUCE: *Makes about 1 cup*

½ cup sugar

¼ cup rice vinegar or distilled white vinegar

2 tablespoons chopped roasted peanuts

2 tablespoons light soy sauce

1 tablespoon chopped red chilies (Thai, serrano, or jalapeño)

1 tablespoon finely minced garlic

1 teaspoon salt

Salads, Snacks, Appetizers

Glass Noodle Salad

Serves 6

This is a noodle dish that has been transformed into a salad. Glass noodles, which are made from mung beans, turn glassy clear when they are cooked. Unlike other noodles, their texture remains elastic even after being tossed with a dressing. Like most Thai salads, the lime taste dominates this refreshing dish.

Place 4 cups of water in a medium saucepan. Bring to a boil over medium heat and add the noodles. Cook, stirring occasionally to separate, until tender, about 5 minutes. Drain and rinse with cold water. Cut the noodles into 6-inch lengths and set aside.

Heat the oil in a skillet. Add the shallots and sauté over medium heat for 3–5 minutes or until light brown and crispy. Do not burn. Remove from the oil and drain on absorbent paper or paper towels.

In the same skillet, sauté the garlic for 2–3 minutes or until fragrant. Add the mushrooms and optional tofu and sauté 3–5 minutes or until the mushrooms are tender. Alternatively, the mushrooms can be poached in boiling water with a little salt.

3–4 ounces dried cellophane noodles or mung bean noodles [*woon sen*]

1/4 cup vegetable oil

1/4 cup thinly sliced shallots

3 tablespoons minced garlic

3 cups coarsely chopped fresh wood ear mushrooms or other mushrooms of your choice

2 cups julienne fried tofu (optional)

1 cup julienne red onions

1 cup sliced Chinese celery, in 2-inch lengths

5 tablespoons fresh lime juice, or more to taste

1/4 cup light soy sauce, or more to taste

3 tablespoons sugar, or more to taste

2 tablespoons chopped fresh Thai chilies, more or less to taste

2 tablespoons chili paste with soybean oil [*namprik pow*]

1 head of lettuce, cleaned and cut into bite-size pieces

1 cup julienne red bell peppers, for garnish

1/4 cup chopped roasted peanuts, for garnish

3 tablespoons chopped fresh cilantro leaves, for garnish

3 tablespoons chopped green onions, for garnish

Combine the noodles, mushrooms, tofu, red onions, celery, lime juice, soy sauce, sugar, Thai chilies, and chili paste with soybean oil in a large bowl. Toss to mix well. Adjust the flavor by adding more soy sauce, lime juice, and sugar to taste.

Line a serving platter with a bed of lettuce. Top with the salad and garnish with the bell peppers, peanuts, cilantro, and green onions just before serving.

Eggplant Salad

Serves 6

Asian eggplants come in many sizes, shapes, and colors, including purple, green, and even bright orange. The firm texture of long purple or green eggplants is better suited for this dish, as the rounder purple eggplants have a less dense and more mushy texture. The eggplants absorb the seasonings well and the flavors penetrate quickly throughout, as if the eggplants had been marinated for a long time.

2 large Asian long eggplants, purple or green

2 large red or yellow chilies (serrano or jalapeño)

¼ cup vegetable oil

¼ cup thinly sliced shallots

½ cup chopped fresh water chestnuts or peeled jicama

¼ cup thinly sliced red onions, in half rings

¼ cup fresh lime juice, or more to taste

3 tablespoons light soy sauce, or more to taste

2 tablespoons sugar, or more to taste

2 tablespoons finely chopped fresh Thai chilies, more or less to taste

1 head of lettuce, cleaned and cut into bite-size pieces

2 tablespoons chopped green onions, for garnish

2 tablespoons chopped fresh cilantro leaves, for garnish

Grill the whole eggplants and chilies over an open flame or place them on a baking sheet and roast them in a preheated 375°F oven for 10–15 minutes or until tender. The skin of the eggplants should be brown and wrinkled and soft enough to be pierced easily with a fork. Let cool; then peel and discard the skin and stems. Cut the eggplants into ½-inch cubes and chop the chilies. Set aside.

Heat the oil in a small skillet over medium heat. Add the sliced shallots and sauté 2–4 minutes or until light brown and crispy. Do not burn. Remove from the pan and drain on absorbent paper or paper towels. Set aside for garnish.

Combine the eggplant, chilies, water chestnuts, red onions, lime juice, soy sauce, sugar, and Thai chilies in a large bowl and mix well. Adjust the seasonings to taste. Line a serving platter with a bed of the lettuce. Top with the eggplant salad and sprinkle with the green onions, cilantro, and fried shallots before serving.

Cucumber Salad

Serves 6

This dish is best served crisp, cold, and crunchy. Ajad plays many roles in Thai meals. It is served as a sauce for crêpes, corn fritters, and fried tofu; as a salad with all types of satay dishes; or as an accompaniment to curries for clearing the palate. It is easy and quick to prepare and its dressing can be kept refrigerated for a few weeks.

Combine the sugar, vinegar, and salt in a small saucepan and place over medium heat. Simmer until the mixture turns into a thin syrup, about 5 minutes. Remove from the heat and let cool completely.

Ten minutes before serving, combine the syrup with the sliced cucumbers and onions and toss well. Transfer to a serving bowl and garnish with the optional peanuts, cilantro, and bell peppers.

1/2 cup sugar

1/2 cup rice vinegar or distilled white vinegar

1 teaspoon salt, or more to taste

2 cups thinly sliced English cucumbers, in half circles

1/2 cup thinly sliced red onions, in half rings

1/4 cup chopped roasted peanuts (optional, for garnish)

3 sprigs fresh cilantro, leaves only, for garnish

1/4 cup julienne bell peppers (orange, red, or yellow, for garnish)

Herb Cups

Serves 6

This is a Thai snack that brings people together—assembling the food, eating, and talking around an array of fresh offerings. The dish persuades guests to eat healthy vegetables and herbs with medicinal properties. The ingredients usually are carefully arranged so everyone can have fun making this self-serve, one-bite snack.

Preheat the oven to 350°F. Place the coconut on a baking tray and roast it in the oven for 10–15 minutes or until light brown and crispy. Watch closely so it does not burn.

Prepare the onions, ginger, and lime, dicing them carefully so they are uniform in shape and size. Stem the spinach and clean the leaves thoroughly. Arrange all the ingredients separately but side by side on a large platter with a bowl of Coconut Syrup Sauce on the side.

Meang Kum

HERB CUPS:

1 $\frac{1}{2}$ cups shredded coconut or coconut flakes (sweetened or unsweetened)

$\frac{1}{2}$ cup finely diced red onions, in $\frac{1}{8}$-inch cubes or smaller

$\frac{1}{2}$ cup peeled and finely diced fresh ginger, in $\frac{1}{8}$-inch cubes or smaller

$\frac{1}{2}$ cup finely diced lime with skin, in $\frac{1}{8}$-inch cubes or smaller

1 bunch spinach, lettuce, or Chinese broccoli leaves, to use as wrappers

2 tablespoons minced fresh chilies (optional)

$\frac{1}{2}$ cup whole roasted peanuts

1 cup Coconut Syrup Sauce (recipe follows)

To prepare a self-serve, bite-size portion, fold a leaf into a cone and fill it halfway with the roasted coconut. Sprinkle with a little of the diced onions, ginger, lime, optional chilies, and peanuts. Top with a teaspoon of the Coconut Syrup Sauce and eat it using your hands.

To make the Coconut Syrup Sauce, toast the coconut, shallots, and galangal in a dry pan over medium heat for 3–5 minutes or until light brown and fragrant.

In a mortar with pestle, grind and pound the roasted coconut, shallots, galangal, and vegetable base, starting with one ingredient and adding one ingredient at a time until the mixture forms a smooth paste. Alternatively, place the coconut, shallots, galangal, and vegetable base in a food processor and blend into a smooth paste.

Combine the paste, palm sugar, water, and soy sauce in a small saucepan. Place over medium heat and simmer for 5–7 minutes or until the mixture reduces to a thick syrup. Cool and serve.

COCONUT SYRUP SAUCE: *Makes about 2 ⅓ cups*

½ cup shredded coconut or coconut flakes

⅓ cup minced shallots

1 tablespoon minced galangal, or 2 tablespoons minced fresh ginger

1 tablespoon vegetable base, or 1 vegetable bouillon cube

¾ cup palm sugar, or more to taste

½ cup water

2 tablespoons soy sauce or soy paste, or more to taste

Salads, Snacks, Appetizers

Lemongrass and Mushroom Salad

Serves 6

Lemongrass is believed to have medicinal properties as an antibacterial; it also is used as a tonic to aid diges- tion. Lemongrass is most popular for infusing a citrus aroma into soup broths and curry pastes. In this recipe, only the tender parts of the fresh lemongrass are sliced thinly and added directly to the salad. Its crunchy tex- ture is surprisingly similar to nuts but with an explosive flavor of aromatic citrus.

3 tablespoons vegetable oil

3 tablespoons thinly sliced shallots

1 1/2 cups sliced portobello mushrooms, cut into long, thin strips

1 1/2 cups sliced oyster mushrooms, cut into long, thin strips

1 1/2 cups sliced button mushrooms

1/4 cup light soy sauce, or more to taste

1/4 cup fresh lime juice, or more to taste

2 tablespoons sugar, or more to taste

2 tablespoons chili paste with soybean oil [*namprik pow*]

1 tablespoon chopped fresh Thai chilies, more or less to taste

1/2 cup sliced red onions, in half rings

1/4 cup thinly sliced lemongrass, tender midsection only

1 head of lettuce or cabbage, cleaned and cut into bite-size pieces

1 cup inoki mushrooms, roots trimmed, for garnish

1/4 cup julienne colored bell peppers (orange, red, or yellow), for garnish

3 tablespoons chopped fresh cilantro leaves, for garnish

2 tablespoons chopped green onions, for garnish

Heat the oil in a skillet. Add the shallots and sauté over medium heat for 2–3 minutes or until light brown and fragrant. Stir in the portobello mushrooms, oyster mushrooms, and button mushrooms, and sauté for 2–3 minutes or until tender. Set aside.

Combine the light soy sauce, lime juice, sugar, chili paste with soybean oil, and Thai chilies in a small bowl. Mix well to make a dressing for the salad.

Just before serving, combine the cooked mushrooms, red onions, and sliced lemongrass in a large bowl. Add the dressing and mix thoroughly. Adjust the flavor with more soy sauce, lime juice, and sugar to taste.

Line a serving platter with a bed of the lettuce and top with the mushroom salad. Garnish with the inoki mushrooms, bell peppers, cilantro, and green onions.

Minced Mushroom Salad

Serves 6

Laab is the local word for preparing a refreshing salad by quickly blending ground meat, fresh herbs, and lime juice. In this recipe, plant-based products, such as mushrooms and seaweeds, are used instead of meat to make a vegetarian meal. Roasted rice provides a smoky aroma that goes well with the earthy essence of the mushrooms. Traditionally, this salad is eaten with sticky rice. An array of fresh vegetables, such as lettuce, cabbage, and long beans, is essential as an accompaniment.

2 tablespoons rice

1 cup diced portobello mushrooms, in ⅛-inch cubes

1 cup diced wood ear mushrooms, in ⅛-inch cubes

1 cup diced oyster mushrooms, in ⅛-inch cubes

1 cup fresh seaweed knots or threads or additional mushrooms of your choice

¼ cup thinly sliced shallots

¼ cup chopped fresh mint leaves

¼ cup light soy sauce, or more to taste

¼ cup fresh lime juice, or more to taste

2 tablespoons sugar, or more to taste

2 tablespoons minced garlic

1 teaspoon dried chili flakes, more or less to taste

1 teaspoon chopped fresh Thai chilies, more or less to taste

¼ cup julienne colored bell peppers (orange, red, or yellow), for garnish

3 tablespoons chopped fresh cilantro leaves, for garnish

2 tablespoons chopped green onions, for garnish

1 head of lettuce or cabbage, cleaned and cut into bite-size pieces

½ cup sliced long beans or green beans, in 1½-inch lengths

Roast the rice in a dry pan over medium heat for 5–7 minutes or until brown and fragrant. In a mortar with pestle, grind and pound the roasted rice until it is coarsely ground. Set aside.

Poach the mushrooms and seaweed in boiling water for 3–5 minutes or until tender. Drain well.

Just before serving, combine the ground rice, mushrooms, seaweed, shallots, mint leaves, soy sauce, lime juice, sugar, garlic, chili flakes, and Thai chilies in a large bowl. Mix thoroughly. Adjust the flavor by adding more soy sauce, lime juice, and sugar to taste.

Transfer to a serving platter and garnish with the bell peppers, cilantro, and green onions. Serve with the lettuce and long beans on the side.

Minced Tofu Salad

Serves 6

This is another refreshing laab. *Silken tofu is used because it readily absorbs the dressing. Thai salad, especially this dish, requires an intense flavor and is served with an array of accompanying fresh vegetables, such as lettuce, cabbage, and long beans.*

2 tablespoons rice

1 1/2 cups firm silken tofu, well drained

2 cups coarsely chopped mushrooms of your choice

1/4 cup chopped fresh mint leaves

1/4 cup light soy sauce, or more to taste

1/4 cup fresh lime juice, or more to taste

2 tablespoons sliced shallots

2 tablespoons sugar, or more to taste

2 teaspoons dried chili flakes

1 teaspoon chopped fresh Thai chilies, more or less to taste

3 tablespoons chopped fresh cilantro leaves, for garnish

2 tablespoons chopped green onions, for garnish

1/4 cup julienne colored bell peppers (orange, red, or yellow), for garnish

1 head of lettuce or cabbage, cleaned and cut into bite-size pieces

1/2 cup sliced long beans or green beans, in 1 1/2-inch lengths

Roast the rice in a dry skillet over medium heat for 5–7 minutes or until brown and fragrant. Transfer to a mortar with pestle and grind and pound the roasted rice until coarsely ground. Set aside.

Crumble the tofu in the same skillet used to roast the rice. Cook and stir over medium heat for 3–5 minutes or until the tofu is dried and light brown. Remove from the heat and set aside.

Poach the mushrooms in boiling water for 3–5 minutes or until tender. Drain and set aside.

Just before serving, combine the ground rice, tofu, mushrooms, mint leaves, soy sauce, lime juice, shallots, sugar, chili flakes, and Thai chilies in a large bowl. Mix gently but thoroughly. Adjust the flavor by adding more soy sauce, lime juice, and sugar to taste.

Transfer to a serving platter and garnish with the cilantro, green onions, and bell peppers. Serve with the lettuce and long beans on the side.

Mini Purses

Serves 6 (40 pieces)

Haw Thong

The ready-made wrappers that are used in this recipe are widely available, including those without eggs such as lumpia, rice paper, and tofu sheets. This dish is a true appetizer, whereas most other Thai appetizers can be eaten as a meal with rice. To achieve the appealing presentation of little purses with tied strings is a time-consuming, delicate process. But the appearance and taste of the end product will impress anyone, including you!

STUFFING:

1 cup chopped water chestnuts or peeled jicama

1 cup chopped bamboo shoots (one 8-ounce can)

1/4 cup chopped fresh cilantro leaves

2 tablespoons cornstarch

1 tablespoon sugar

1 tablespoon minced garlic

1 tablespoon minced fresh cilantro roots or stems

1 tablespoon minced shallots

1 tablespoon soy sauce

1 tablespoon Maggi Seasoning Sauce

1 tablespoon vegetable base, or 1 vegetable bouillon cube

1/4 teaspoon pepper

WRAPPERS AND TIES:

1 bunch garlic chives, or 1 leek, for string ties

1 package thin wonton or lumpia wrappers (3 1/2–4 inches square)

4 cups vegetable oil, for deep frying

Combine all the stuffing ingredients in a food processor. Pulse several times until well mixed but not smooth.

Trim the chives or leek, using the leafy green portions only. For the leek, slice into thin, long strips. Blanch the chives or leek strips in boiling water for just a few seconds to soften them. Rinse with cold water and set aside to drain.

Fill each wrapper with 3/4 teaspoon of stuffing and pull all corners up to form a little purse. Tie and secure the purse with a chive or leek string. Continue the process until all the stuffing has been used.

Place the oil in a deep pan and heat to 375°F. The oil should have a depth of at least two inches. Gently drop the purses into the pan to fit loosely. Deep-fry, stirring occasionally, for 3–5 minutes or until golden brown. Remove from the oil and drain on absorbent paper or paper towels.

Serve the mini purses with Cucumber Salad *Ajad*, page 67, or ready-made Thai sweet chili sauce.

Salads, Snacks, Appetizers

Mushroom Satay

Serves 6

The texture of mushrooms makes them ideal for marinating and skewering. Use your favorite type of mushroom or several different types for a medley of flavors and textures. Not only does Thai cuisine borrow the seasonings of the Spice Islands, it also has adopted the popular dish "satay"—food on skewers—from Indonesia. To make the satay more original, Thais add local herbs and spices and serve the satay with the Thai version of peanut sauce.

2 pounds assorted mushrooms (portobello, shiitake, and button)

1 package bamboo sticks (skewers)

1/4 cup finely minced lemongrass, tender midsection only

3 tablespoons finely minced garlic

3 tablespoons finely minced fresh ginger

3 tablespoons finely minced green onions

1 tablespoon pepper

1 teaspoon salt

Vegetable oil as needed

Slice the large mushrooms into long strips about ½-inch thick. Leave the small mushrooms whole. Skewer the mushrooms horizontally with the bamboo sticks.

To make an herb rub, combine the lemongrass, garlic, ginger, green onions, pepper, and salt in a mortar with pestle or in a food processor until well blended. Rub the herb mixture over the mushrooms, making sure that all surfaces are well covered.

Arrange the skewered mushrooms on a tray, stacking the skewers on top of each other. Sprinkle lightly with the oil. Cover the mushrooms with plastic wrap and refrigerate them overnight. If you are in a hurry, you can marinate them for at least 1 hour at room temperature.

About 30 minutes before you are ready to serve the mushrooms, light a charcoal grill. When it reaches medium heat, grill the mushrooms 2–3 minutes on each side or until they are tender. If the mushrooms seem dry, brush them occasionally with oil.

Serve the Mushroom Satay with Chili Sweet Soy, page 42, or Peanut Sauce, page 48.

Pad Thai Salad

Serves 6

Here is a fresh salad dish with pad thai's characteristic sweet-and-sour flavor. More varieties of fresh and cooked vegetables of your choice could be added. Any type of cooked noodles at room temperature could be incorporated, if you like. Feel free to make a large batch of the dressing and keep it in the refrigerator for another meal. The dressing also can be used as the stir-fry sauce for Pad Thai, page 117.

Combine the fried tofu, bean sprouts, bell peppers, celery, garlic chives, shallots, and garlic in a large bowl. Toss with a small amount of Pad Thai Dressing (recipe follows), and gradually add more to taste.

Arrange a bed of the lettuce on a serving platter and top with the salad. Garnish with the chopped roasted peanuts and cilantro leaves.

To make the dressing, combine all the ingredients in a bowl and stir until the sugar is dissolved.

PAD THAI SALAD:

2 cups julienne fried tofu

2 cups bean sprouts

1 cup julienne colored bell peppers (red, orange, or yellow)

1 cup thinly sliced celery

¼ cup sliced garlic chives or green onions, in 1 ½-inch lengths

3 tablespoons thinly sliced shallots

2 tablespoons thinly sliced garlic

1 head of romaine lettuce, cleaned and cut into thin strips

½ cup chopped roasted peanuts, for garnish

5 sprigs fresh cilantro, leaves only, for garnish

PAD THAI DRESSING:

¼ cup light soy sauce, or more to taste

¼ cup sugar

2 tablespoons finely minced preserved turnips (optional)

2 tablespoons tamarind liquid

2 tablespoons fresh lime juice, or more to taste

2 tablespoons rice vinegar or distilled white vinegar

2 tablespoons vegetable oil (optional)

1 tablespoon paprika or chili powder

1 tablespoon minced fresh red Thai chilies, more or less to taste

Pineapple Coconut Noodles

Serves 6

Pineapple and coconut are a perfect pair for both food and drink in many cuisines. Each fruit has a unique but opposite flavor. With the attraction of opposites, they have been put together deliciously in my favorite childhood dish, which was a popular offering of wandering merchants. Its taste of sweet, creamy coconut and refreshing pineapple will explode in your mouth. On a hot day, or on any day, this fresh dish with mint leaves will calm and soothe you. (See photo, facing page 129.)

COCONUT "SOUR NAM" SAUCE:

1 1/2 cups coconut milk

1 pound silken tofu, well drained and crumbled

1 tablespoon light soy sauce

1 tablespoon vegetable base, or 1 vegetable bouillon cube

1/2 teaspoon salt

1 1/2 cups coconut cream

NOODLES AND GARNISHES:

14–16 ounces dried rice noodles [*kanom jeen*] or Japanese somen noodles

3 cups diced fresh pineapple, in 1/4-inch cubes (about 1 small pineapple)

1/2 cup julienne fresh ginger

1/4 cup chopped fresh mint leaves

2 tablespoons thinly sliced garlic, cut paper thin

2 tablespoons chopped fresh Thai chilies, more or less to taste

1/2 cup light soy sauce

1/2 cup fresh lime juice

1/2 cup sugar

Heat the coconut milk in a medium saucepan over medium heat. When hot, stir in the crumbled tofu, mixing well.

Add the soy sauce, vegetable base, and salt and bring to a boil. Stir in the coconut cream and return to a boil. Remove from the heat and let cool.

Cook the noodles in 6 cups of boiling water until tender, about 5 minutes. Drain and rinse with cold water. Portion the noodles into 3-ounce small wads, each about the size of a small bird's nest, and set aside.

Arrange the pineapple, ginger, mint leaves, garlic, and Thai chilies separately, side by side, on a large serving platter, accompanied by a large bowl of the Coconut "Sour Nam" Sauce and small bowls of soy sauce, lime juice, and sugar.

To self-serve, place 2–3 wads of noodles on a serving plate and pour about ¾ cup of the Coconut "Sour Nam" Sauce over them. Top with ⅓ cup diced pineapple and a little of the ginger, mint leaves, garlic, and chilies. Sprinkle with a little soy sauce, lime juice, and sugar. Toss gently to combine well.

Spicy Green Mango Salad

Serves 6

Sam Gler *means three good friends: green mango, carrots, and cabbage, which are combined to create this sumptuous dish. If you prefer, the carrots and cabbage can be poached, instead of served fresh, to retain their original flavors before being mixed with an aromatic, refreshing dressing. Namprik pow (chili paste with soybean oil) is essential for its pungent and smoky chili flavor.*

SPICY GREEN MANGO SALAD:

2 cups shredded peeled green mango (1 unripe firm mango) or Granny Smith apple

2 cups shredded carrots

2 cups shredded cabbage

1 cup julienne fried tofu (optional)

1 head of lettuce, cleaned and cut into bite-size pieces

1/2 cup chopped roasted peanuts, for garnish

1/4 cup julienne red bell peppers, for garnish

3 sprigs cilantro, leaves only, for garnish

DRESSING:

1/4 cup light soy sauce

1/4 cup tamarind liquid

2 tablespoons chili sauce with soybean oil [*namprik pow*], or more to taste

1 tablespoon sugar

1/4 cup fresh lime juice

1 tablespoon chopped fresh Thai chilies (optional)

Combine the green mango, carrots, cabbage, and optional fried tofu in a large bowl. Toss with a small amount of the dressing (recipe follows), adding a little more to taste.

Line a serving platter with a bed of the lettuce and top with the salad. Sprinkle with the chopped peanuts. Garnish with the red bell peppers and cilantro before serving. Serve the remaining dressing on the side.

Alternatively, decoratively arrange all the ingredients side by side on a serving platter or in different compartments, like a Western chef's salad, and serve the dressing on the side.

To make the dressing, combine the soy sauce, tamarind liquid, chili paste with soybean oil, and sugar in a small saucepan and place over medium heat. Bring to a boil and simmer just long enough to dissolve the sugar. Remove from the heat and let cool. Stir in the lime juice and optional Thai chilies.

Rice Salad

Serves 4

Khao Yum

Healthful and delicious, this salad is a good source of dietary fiber and many vitamins and minerals from various kinds of vegetables. It even incorporates the antibacterial medicinal benefits of lemongrass, galangal, and kaffir lime. Yet the dish has no fat and hardly any cooking is required. It can easily be considered a Thai chef's salad made with local ingredients and a snappy, tasty dressing.

Preheat the oven to 350°F. Place the shredded coconut in a pan and roast in the oven, stirring occasionally, for 5–7 minutes or until light brown and crispy. Remove from the pan and set aside.

Peel the outer shell of the lemongrass and cut off the hard root. Slice the tender midsection crosswise into very thin rings. Stack the kaffir lime leaves and roll them into a tight cigarette-like roll. Thinly slice across the roll and unravel into long, thin strips.

RICE SALAD:

1 cup shredded coconut or coconut flakes (sweetened or unsweetened)

2 stalks lemongrass, tender midsection only, thinly sliced

5 whole kaffir lime leaves, shredded

2 cups steamed rice

1 cup diced fried tofu, in $1/4$-inch cubes

1 cup seeded pomelo or grapefruit segments

1 cup bean sprouts

$1/2$ cup julienne peeled green mango or Granny Smith apple

$1/2$ cup julienne star fruit

$1/2$ cup long beans, finely sliced crosswise

$1/2$ cup thinly sliced English cucumbers, in half circles

Arrange all of the ingredients on a serving platter, side by side, and serve with a bowl of Rice Salad Dressing (recipe follows). To serve, spoon the salad ingredients onto individual plates and sprinkle with the dressing to taste. Toss to mix well before eating.

To make the Rice Salad Dressing, combine all the ingredients in a small saucepan and place over medium heat. Simmer for 15–20 minutes, until the mixture turns into a thick syrup. Strain the dressing through a fine sieve (discard the solids).

RICE SALAD DRESSING: *Nam Boodoo*

2 cups water
1/2 cup palm sugar, grated and packed
1/4 cup chopped shallots
1/4 cup soybean paste or fermented bean curds
2 tablespoons chopped lemongrass, tender midsection only
2 tablespoons chopped galangal
2 tablespoons chopped garlic
2 tablespoons light soy sauce
3 whole kaffir lime leaves

Salads, Snacks, Appetizers

Steamed Stuffed Cabbage

Serves 4

This dish is quite attractive, as it is served in its own edible bowl! White, green, and red cabbage can be used for a kaleidoscope of colors.

1 head medium green, red, or white cabbage
1 cup julienne firm tofu
1 cup julienne shiitake mushrooms
1 tablespoon cornstarch
1 tablespoon sugar
1 tablespoon light soy sauce
1 tablespoon vegetarian stir-fry sauce or Maggi Seasoning Sauce
1/4 teaspoon salt
1/4 teaspoon pepper
1/4 cup thinly sliced red jalapeño peppers or red bell peppers, for garnish
3 sprigs fresh cilantro, for garnish

Carve around the center of the cabbage and scoop out the stem, core, and leaves to create a bowl with a one-inch-thick edge. Reserve ½ cup of the cabbage leaves, sliced into thin strips.

Place the cabbage bowl in a steamer rack over boiling water. Cover tightly and steam for 7–10 minutes or until tender. Remove from the heat and immediately plunge the cabbage bowl into a bowl or sink filled with cold water. When the cabbage bowl has cooled completely, remove it from the water and set it aside, upside down, to drain.

Combine the reserved ½ cup cabbage leaves, tofu, mushrooms, cornstarch, sugar, soy sauce, stir-fry sauce, salt, and pepper in a medium bowl and mix well. Stuff the mixture into the cabbage bowl, mounding it high.

Return the stuffed cabbage to the steamer and steam 10–15 minutes or until the stuffing is hot and firm. Garnish with the red peppers and cilantro before serving.

Vegetable Satay

Serves 6

Not only have Thais borrowed many of the spices from the Spice Islands, they also adopted the popular dish satay—food on skewers—from Indonesia. To make the satay more original, Thais add local herbs and spices and serve it with the Thai version of peanut sauce. (See photo, facing page 160.)

2 tablespoons chopped shallots

1 tablespoon chopped garlic

1 tablespoon chopped galangal

1 tablespoon chopped lemongrass, tender midsection only

1/4 cup vegetable oil

2 tablespoons sugar

1 teaspoon salt

1 package bamboo skewers, soaked in cold water

1 cup diced colored bell peppers (red, orange, or yellow), in 2-inch squares

1 cup diced onions, in 2-inch squares

1 cup diced mushrooms of your choice, in 2-inch squares

1 cup diced zucchini, in 2-inch squares

1 cup diced Asian eggplants, in 2-inch squares

1/4 cup coconut cream or vegetable oil (optional)

Using a mortar with pestle or a food processor, blend the shallots, garlic, galangal, and lemongrass until they form a smooth paste.

Combine the paste with the oil, sugar, and salt in a large bowl. Add the vegetables and toss until they are evenly coated. Let marinate for at least 30 minutes.

Soak the bamboo sticks in water to help prevent them from burning. Skewer the vegetables with the bamboo sticks.

Thirty minutes before you are ready to cook the satay, light a firewood or charcoal grill. Grill the vegetables over medium heat, brushing them with the optional coconut cream or oil and turning them occasionally until they are evenly tender, about 5 minutes on each side.

Serve the satay with Peanut Sauce, page 48, or Chili Sweet Soy, page 42.

Tofu Patties

Serves 6

The right combination of ingredients and the proper mixing technique are crucial for these patties to be crunchy on the outside and soft and crumbly in the inside. Please pay careful attention when mixing the batter; it should hold together loosely with small chunks of ingredients in between. A mushy, paste-like batter won't allow the hot oil to seep through, resulting in gluey, uncooked patties.

1 cup chopped water chestnuts

1 cup sliced fresh wood ear mushrooms (or 1/2 cup dried wood ear mushrooms)

1 cup firm silken tofu, well drained and crumbled

1/4 cup dried lily buds

1/4 cup preserved turnips

1/4 cup all-purpose flour

2 tablespoons cornstarch

1 tablespoon chopped shallots

1 tablespoon vegetable base, or 1 vegetable bouillon cube, finely crumbled

1/2 teaspoon pepper

1/2 teaspoon salt

3 cups vegetable oil, for frying

If using fresh water chestnuts, peel and chop them into small chunks. If using dried wood ear mushrooms, soak them in warm water until fully expanded. Drain and slice into fine, thin strips.

If the tofu was packed in water, place it in a strainer to drain off the water completely. Crumble into small chunks and set aside.

Soak the lily buds and preserved turnips in warm water to soften and remove excess salt. Drain and finely chop into small chunks.

Combine the water chestnuts, mushrooms, lily buds, turnips, flour, cornstarch, shallots, vegetable base, pepper, and salt in a food processor. Pulse the mixture several times until it is well mixed but still has small chunks. Do not process into a fine paste. Transfer to a bowl and gently fold in the tofu. The texture should be similar to crumbly cookie dough. Add a little water if needed to hold the mixture together.

Heat the oil in a pan or skillet to 375°F for deep-frying. The oil should be at least two inches deep. With damp hands, lightly form the mixture into small patties, one-quarter-inch thick and about one inch in diameter. Gently drop them in the pan to fit loosely.

Fry the patties, turning once, for 3–5 minutes or until they are golden brown on both sides. Remove from the oil and drain on absorbent paper or paper towels. Serve the patties with Cucumber Salad *Ajad*, page 67, or ready-made Thai sweet chili sauce.

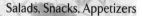

Vegetarian Spiced Pockets

Serves 6 (about 40 pieces)

This recipe provides two types of wrappers and cooking techniques: thin wonton skins for deep-frying, and puff pastry sheets for baking. The filling is the same with either method, and it can also be served as a main dish over rice without any wrapping.

Heat the oil in a large saucepan over medium heat. Add the shallots, garlic, and ginger. Sauté for 3 minutes or until fragrant. Add the potatoes, carrots, and corn, and stir to mix well.

Stir in the water, curry powder, soy sauce, sugar, vegetable base, and pepper. Reduce the heat and simmer for 7–10 minutes or until the vegetables are almost tender. Remove from the heat and stir in the green onions and mint. Let cool completely. The mixture should be fairly dry for stuffing.

Place about 1 tablespoon of stuffing in the middle of a wonton wrapper. Apply water lightly around the edges and fold in half to seal completely into a triangular or half circle. Fill the remaining wrappers in the same way until all the stuffing is used.

FILLING:

2 tablespoons vegetable oil

3 tablespoons minced shallots

2 tablespoons minced garlic

2 tablespoons minced fresh ginger

1 cup diced potatoes, in $1/8$-inch cubes

1 cup diced carrots, in $1/8$-inch cubes

1 cup fresh corn kernels

$1/4$ cup water

2 tablespoons curry powder

2 tablespoons light soy sauce

2 tablespoons sugar

1 tablespoon vegetable base, or 1 vegetable bouillon cube

1 teaspoon pepper

3 tablespoons chopped green onions

3 tablespoons chopped fresh mint leaves

WRAPPERS: Deep-Frying

1 package (14 ounces) ready-made thin wonton or lumpia wrappers, $3 1/2$–4 inches square or round

4 cups vegetable oil, for deep-frying

DEEP-FRYING

Place the oil in a deep pan and heat to 375°F. The oil should have a depth of at least two inches. Gently drop several stuffed wontons into the pan to fit loosely. Fry 2–3 minutes, turning occasionally, until golden brown on all sides. Remove from the oil and drain on absorbent paper or paper towels.

Serve as a snack or appetizer with Cucumber Salad *Ajad*, page 67, or ready-made Thai sweet chili sauce.

WRAPPERS: Baking

1 package frozen puff pastry dough
   (four 8 x 10-inch sheets)
1 tablespoon dark soy sauce
1 tablespoon rice vinegar
1 tablespoon water
2 tablespoons black sesame seeds or poppy seeds

BAKING

Thaw the puff pastry sheets completely. Preheat the oven to 375°F. Oil a baking sheet and set it aside.

Spread out a sheet of the pastry dough and cut it in half lengthwise into 4-inch wide strips. Fill the length of each strip, along one edge, with the filling, forming a log to cover about one-quarter of the width. Apply water lightly on the other edge.

Wrap and roll the pastry tightly and seal it completely. Cut across the roll into 1-inch, bite-size pieces. (Before cutting, if the rolls are too soft, refrigerate for 15 minutes to firm up the dough for easier handling.)

Arrange the pieces on the prepared baking sheet. Leave enough room between them so they do not touch.

Combine the dark soy sauce, vinegar, and water. Lightly brush the surface of the pastries with this mixture, and sprinkle with the black sesame seeds. Bake 15–20 minutes or until golden brown.

Serve with Cucumber Salad *Ajad*, page 67, or ready-made Thai sweet chili sauce.

Salads, Snacks, Appetizers

Green Salad with Peanut Dressing

Serves 6

Salad Kaek

Thai food was originally a fusion of its many neighboring influences. This fresh salad is an amalgamation of many cuisines: Chinese, Indian, Indonesian, and now American with its popular peanut butter. Many types of fresh and cooked vegetables provide a variety of flavors and textures.

Place 2 cups of water with a little salt in a small saucepan. Bring to a boil, add the diced potatoes, and cook 3–5 minutes or until tender. Drain and rinse under cold water to completely cool; set aside. Refill the same saucepan with water. Bring to a boil and blanch the bean sprouts until tender, about 1 minute. Drain and set aside.

Arrange the potatoes, bean sprouts, lettuce pieces, cucumbers, red onions, and tomatoes on a serving platter. Top with the julienne tofu. To serve, place portions of the salad on serving plates and top with Peanut Dressing (recipe follows) and the potato chips.

GREEN SALAD:

1 cup peeled diced potatoes or sweet potatoes, in ¼-inch cubes

2 cups bean sprouts

1 head of lettuce, cleaned and cut into bite-size pieces

1 cup thinly sliced English cucumbers, in half circles

½ cup thinly sliced red onions, in half rings

½ cup julienne seeded tomatoes

1 cup julienne fried or firm tofu

1 (6-ounce) bag unsalted potato chips

PEANUT DRESSING: *(Makes about 3½ cups)*

1 cup coconut milk

¼ cup Red Curry Paste, page 50, or 2 tablespoons ready-made red curry paste

½ cup peanut paste or chunky peanut butter

⅓ cup palm sugar, or more to taste

¼ cup light soy sauce, or more to taste

¼ cup tamarind liquid

1 cup coconut cream

1 tablespoon fresh lime juice, or more to taste

To make the Peanut Dressing, place ½ cup of the coconut milk in a small saucepan. Stir in the curry paste and cook over medium heat for 2–4 minutes or until fragrant. Add the remaining ½ cup coconut milk, peanut paste, palm sugar, soy sauce, and tamarind liquid. Stir constantly for 3–5 minutes or until the mixture is well combined and heated through. Remove from the heat and stir in the coconut cream and lime juice. Adjust the seasonings to taste. Add a small amount water if the dressing is too thick.

Hot and Sour Soups and Plain Broths

Thai soup *tom* is a light soup that does not contain curry paste. Thais consider most curries to be soups. Curries, on the other hand, contain a spicy curry paste and come in a variety of consistencies, from watery to semi-dry to dry. They may or may not contain coconut milk. *Tom* may also be made with or without coconut milk, but all *tom* are thin and do not contain curry paste. However, tom can be very hot and spicy if chilies are added.

There generally are two kinds of soup: hot and sour *tom yum* and plain broth *tom juud*. The hot and sour is very liquidy (*tom*) and mimics the flavors of Thai salad (*yum*), hence the name *tom yum*. Plain broths or broth with a coconut milk base are used liberally in *tom yum*. Herbs and spices (such as lemongrass and galangal) are used to flavor the broth before the meats or, in our case, vegetables are added. For a refreshing taste, the salt, and especially the sweet, sour, and hot chilies, and the lime juice are added last, after everything else is cooked. Overcooked lime juice would dull its freshness, and overcooked chilies, once their oils are broken down, would permeate the soup broth with their overpowering heat. Working with the final seasonings often becomes a juggling act to attain the correct balance of sour and salt to make the soup delicious.

Plain broth *tom juud* is a good example that proves that Thai food does not necessarily have to be hot. To the surprise of many, a lot of Thai people cannot tolerate the heat of chilies. *Tom juud* is a staple for those Thais and others who seek refuge from hot chilies. It can also be a soothing accompaniment to help quell the fire of a spicy dish. Vegetables are added to the plain soup broth and then seasoned with a few herbs and spices, but no chilies or lime juice. A degree of spiciness can be attained with just a shake of ground white pepper.

Assorted Vegetable Stew

Serves 6

There is no dish easier to make than this one—just prepare the vegetables, add the seasonings, and cook for thirty minutes. If possible, the stew should be cooked in advance and reheated, as its flavor improves over time. Leftover vegetables are ideal for this dish.

Combine all the ingredients in a large saucepan. Place over medium-low heat and simmer until all the vegetables are tender, about 30 minutes. Serve hot by itself or with steamed rice.

8 cups vegetable stock or water

1 cup diced fried or firm tofu, in 1/2-inch cubes (optional)

1 cup sliced tofu sheets or skins, in bite-size pieces

1 cup chopped cabbage, in bite-size pieces

1 cup cauliflower florets

1 cup sliced Chinese broccoli [*gai lan*], in bite-size pieces

1 cup sliced baby bok choy, in bite-size pieces

1 cup Chinese celery, in 1-inch pieces

1 cup sliced black mushrooms, soaked in warm water, in bite-size pieces

1 cup diced daikon (or other vegetable of your choice), in 1/2-inch cubes (optional)

3 tablespoons light soy sauce, or more to taste

2 tablespoons brown sugar

2 tablespoons Chinese five-spice powder (optional)

2 tablespoons sweet soy sauce

2 tablespoons Maggi Seasoning Sauce

1 tablespoon vegetable base, or 1 vegetable bouillon cube

1 teaspoon pepper

Salt

Galangal Coconut Soup

Serves 6

Instead of ginger, which is widely used in almost all Asian cooking, Thais also use galangal, a local ingredient, to spice up their cuisine. Galangal provides such a unique flavor that there is no substitute for it. It is widely available in fresh, dried, and frozen forms in Asian grocery stores. This recipe highlights the best and most popular use of galangal, paring it with coconut milk and mushrooms. The combination of ingredients in this aromatic, creamy soup, with its refreshing sweet-and-sour taste, makes the dish one of the top ten choices of both Thais and lovers of Thai food.

3 cups vegetable stock

6 pieces thinly sliced fresh galangal (about a 1 x 1-inch piece)

2 stalks lemongrass, cut into several 2-inch-long pieces and bruised

4 whole kaffir lime leaves

4 cups sliced assorted mushrooms, in bite-size pieces

1/4 cup thinly sliced shallots

2 cups coconut milk

3 tablespoons light soy sauce, or more to taste

2 tablespoons sugar

1 tablespoon vegetable base, or 1 vegetable bouillon cube

1/4 cup fresh lime juice, or more to taste

1 teaspoon chopped fresh Thai chilies, more or less to taste

2 tablespoons chopped fresh cilantro leaves, for garnish

2 tablespoons chopped green onions, for garnish

Bring the stock to a boil in a medium saucepan. Add the galangal, lemongrass, and kaffir lime leaves. Simmer for 10–15 minutes or until the broth is reduced by one-quarter to one-half the original volume. Strain and discard the solids or leave them in for a stronger flavor.

Add the mushrooms and shallots and simmer 2–3 minutes or until the mushrooms are tender. Stir in the coconut milk, soy sauce, sugar, and vegetable base. Bring to a boil and remove from the heat.

Stir in the lime juice and Thai chilies. Adjust the flavor by adding more soy sauce and lime juice to taste. Transfer to individual bowls and garnish with the cilantro and green onions before serving.

Bamboo Shoot Stew

Serves 4

Wandering merchants usually offer this dish on the streets of Thailand. The original recipe came from China and was considered to be hearty and healthful, similar to chicken soup for a cold. It can be a light meal or a snack just to help carry you through until the next major meal. Fresh bamboo shoots are hard to find in the United States. Their tough outer sheaths are stripped away and the tender shoots are cooked in several changes of water to rid them of any bitterness.

Place the vegetable stock in a medium saucepan and bring to a boil. Add the soy sauce, sugar, and vegetable base.

Stir in the bamboo shoots, baby corn, carrots, mushrooms, and tofu sheets. Cook 7–10 minutes or until the vegetables are tender. (If using canned products, drain the brine and cook in boiling water for 3 minutes to refresh the flavors.)

Dissolve the cornstarch in the ¼ cup cold water and stir this mixture into the simmering soup. Stir constantly until the mixture thickens slightly, about 5 minutes. Adjust the flavor with more seasonings to taste. Ladle the stew into serving bowls and sprinkle with the pepper, cilantro, and green onions. Serve with Chili Vinegar Sauce (recipe follows) or bottled chili sauce [*sambal olek*] on the side as a condiment.

BAMBOO SHOOT STEW:

5 cups vegetable stock

3 tablespoons light soy sauce, or more to taste

1 tablespoon sugar, or more to taste

1 tablespoon vegetable base, or 1 vegetable bouillon cube

2 cups julienne bamboo shoots

1 cup thinly sliced baby corn

1 cup diced carrots, in ¼-inch cubes

1 cup thinly sliced mushrooms of your choice

1 cup fresh tofu sheets or skins, in bite-size pieces

3 tablespoons cornstarch, or more as needed

¼ cup cold water

1 teaspoon pepper

¼ cup chopped fresh cilantro leaves, for garnish

¼ cup chopped green onions, for garnish

½ cup Chili Vinegar Sauce (recipe follows) or chili sauce [*sambal olek*], for an accompaniment

CHILI VINEGAR SAUCE:

3 fresh red jalapeño or serrano peppers, finely minced

¼ cup distilled white vinegar

1 tablespoon finely minced garlic

½ teaspoon salt

To make the Chili Vinegar Sauce, combine all the ingredients in a bowl. Alternatively, combine the peppers, garlic, and salt in a mortar with pestle, and pound until well blended. Transfer to a bowl and stir in the vinegar.

Vegetable Stock

Makes 6 cups

Stock or broth in any kind of soup is the key to a delicious flavor. A good, flavorful stock contributes a great deal to the success of the dish. There are many ways to produce a good stock from various types of fresh vegetables. This simple recipe consistently gives excellent results. Make it in large batches and freeze it so you always have some on hand.

Combine all the ingredients in a large pot and bring to a boil. Reduce the heat to medium-low and simmer for 30–45 minutes or until all the vegetables begin to disintegrate. Pour through a fine sieve and discard the solids.

Nam Soup

12 cups water
1 onion, chopped
1 leek, cleaned and chopped
1 carrot, chopped
1 stalk celery, chopped
1 daikon radish or other vegetable of your choice, chopped
1/2 cup chopped fresh cilantro roots and stems
2 tablespoons chopped garlic (optional)
1 teaspoon course pepper
1 teaspoon salt (optional)

Soups and Broths

Glass Noodle Soup

Serves 4

This is another soup that is cooked frequently in Thai households in addition to the popular hot-and-sour soup tom yum. *It is the equivalent of noodle soup in the United States. Broth soup* tom juud *proves that Thai food does not necessarily have to be hot. Tom juud is a staple for those Thais and others who seek refuge from hot chilies. It can also be a soothing accompaniment to help quell the fire of a spicy dish. It is easy and quick to make and it complements all other dishes in a meal, especially ones that are comprised of only dry ingredients.*

2 ounces dried cellophane, glass, or mung bean noodles

4–5 dried black mushroom caps

1/4 cup dried lily buds

2 tablespoons vegetable oil

3 tablespoons thinly sliced shallots

5 cups vegetable stock

2 tablespoons Chinese cooking wine [*shu shang*] or sherry wine

2 tablespoons light soy sauce, or more to taste

1 tablespoon Maggi Seasoning Sauce

1 tablespoon sugar

1/2 teaspoon white pepper

Salt

2 cups thinly sliced baby bok choy (about 1/2 pound)

1 cup sliced Chinese celery, in 1 1/2-inch lengths

1 cup diced soft tofu, in 1/8-inch cubes

2 tablespoons chopped fresh cilantro, for garnish

2 tablespoons chopped green onions, for garnish

Soak the dried noodles, mushroom caps, and lily buds separately in warm water until they are fully soft and expanded, about 15 minutes. Drain and lightly squeeze dry. Cut the noodles into 6-inch strands and thinly slice the mushroom caps.

Place the oil in a small skillet over medium heat. Add the shallots and fry 3–5 minutes or until light brown and crispy. Do not burn. Remove from the skillet and drain on absorbent paper or paper towels. Set aside for garnish.

Place the vegetable stock in a medium saucepan and bring to a boil over medium heat. Add the wine, soy sauce, Maggi Seasoning Sauce, sugar, pepper, and salt to taste. Bring to a boil and add the noodles, mushroom caps, lily buds, bok choy, Chinese celery, and tofu. Simmer 5–7 minutes or until the vegetables are tender. Remove from the heat.

Ladle the soup into individual bowls and sprinkle with the reserved fried shallots. Garnish with the chopped cilantro and green onions before serving.

Hot-and-Sour Lemongrass Soup

Serves 6

Tom yum is the most common dish cooked in Thai households, where most fresh herbs and spices can be gathered from the backyard garden. It is quick and easy to prepare, and any seasoning can be added at any time, according to taste. If all else fails and you are in a time crunch, tom yum can save the day.

5 cups vegetable stock

3 stalks lemongrass, cut into several 2-inch-long pieces and bruised

5 pieces thinly sliced galangal (about a 1 x 1-inch piece)

5 whole kaffir lime leaves

2 tablespoons thinly sliced shallots

1 tablespoon chopped garlic

3 cups sliced oyster mushrooms or other mushrooms of your choice, in bite-size pieces

2 cups sliced firm tofu, in bite-size pieces

1/4 cup light soy sauce, or more to taste

1 tablespoon chili paste with soybean oil [*namprik pow*]

5 whole fresh Thai chilies, bruised, more or less to taste

1/4 cup fresh lime juice, or more to taste

2 tablespoons chopped fresh cilantro, for garnish

2 tablespoons chopped green onions, for garnish

Place the stock in a medium saucepan and bring to a boil. Add the lemongrass, galangal, kaffir leaves, shallots, and garlic. Simmer for 5 minutes to extract the flavors from the herbs.

Stir in the mushrooms, tofu, soy sauce, and chili paste with soybean oil. Simmer until the mushrooms are tender, about 5 minutes. Remove from the heat and stir in the Thai chilies and lime juice. Adjust the flavor by adding more soy sauce, lime juice, and chili paste with soybean oil to taste.

Ladle the soup into individual bowls and garnish with the cilantro and green onions before serving.

Hunter Soup

Serves 6

Every cuisine seems to have its own so-called "hunter" dish, since the hunter also has to eat (some are even good cooks). This vegetarian version is easy to prepare and delivers a surprisingly hearty soup full of aromatic flavors. A variety of vegetables can be added in an appropriate order, taking into consideration their cooking time.

2 tablespoons vegetable oil

1/3 cup Hunter Curry Paste *Gaeng Paa*, page 45, or 3 tablespoons ready-made paste

1 1/2 cups sliced long beans or green beans, in 1 1/2-inch lengths

1 1/2 cups julienne carrots or Asian eggplants

1 1/2 cups peeled and diced kabocha squash or pumpkin, in 1/2-inch cubes

4 cups vegetable stock or water

2 cups sliced assorted mushrooms of your choice

2 tablespoons light soy sauce, or more to taste

1 tablespoon vegetable base, or 1 vegetable bouillon cube

1/2 cup holy basil leaves [*bai kaprow*]

1/4 cup thinly sliced red jalapeño or bell peppers, for garnish

Place the oil in a medium saucepan over medium heat. Add the curry paste and cook 2–3 minutes or until fragrant. Add the long beans, carrots, and kabocha squash, and mix until the vegetables are evenly coated with the curry paste.

Add the stock and bring to a boil. Simmer 5–7 minutes or until the vegetables are almost tender. Stir in the mushrooms, soy sauce, and vegetable base. Bring the mixture to a boil one more time. Adjust the flavor by adding more soy sauce to taste.

Remove from the heat and sprinkle with the basil leaves and red peppers before serving hot with steamed rice.

Rice Porridge Soup

Khao Tom King

Rice porridge soup is a popular breakfast dish for Thai people. It has a mild flavor and soft texture that is light and easy to digest. Leftover steamed rice is often used. This dish is not only suitable for breakfast but also as a light meal after a heavy drinking spree.

3 tablespoons vegetable oil

3 tablespoons thinly sliced garlic

3 tablespoons julienne fresh ginger

2 tablespoons finely minced fresh cilantro roots or stems

2 tablespoons finely minced garlic

8 cups vegetable stock

2 cups steamed rice

3 tablespoons light soy sauce, or more to taste

1 tablespoon Maggi Seasoning Sauce

1 tablespoon vegetable base, or 1 vegetable bouillon cube

1 tablespoon sugar

2 cups julienne fried or firm tofu

2 cups Chinese celery, in 1 1/2-inch lengths

1 teaspoon pepper, for garnish

3 tablespoons chopped fresh cilantro leaves, for garnish

3 tablespoons chopped green onions, for garnish

1/2 cup rice vinegar or distilled white vinegar, for accompaniment

1/4 cup sliced jalapeño or serrano peppers, in thin rings, for accompaniment

Place the oil in a medium saucepan over medium heat. Add the sliced garlic and fry 3–5 minutes or until light brown and crispy. Do not burn. Strain and remove from the hot oil. Drain on absorbent paper or paper towels and set aside for garnish.

Add the ginger, cilantro roots, and garlic to the saucepan and sauté for 3 minutes or until the garlic is light brown and fragrant. Add the stock and bring to a boil.

Stir in the steamed rice, light soy sauce, Maggi Seasoning Sauce, vegetable base, and sugar. Bring to a boil.

Stir in the tofu and Chinese celery. Bring the mixture to a boil one more time and remove from the heat.

Ladle the soup into serving bowls and garnish with the fried garlic, pepper, cilantro, and green onions.

Combine the vinegar and jalapeño peppers in a small bowl. Serve on the side as an accompaniment. Sprinkle over the rice soup for extra sour-and-spicy flavor.

Stuffed Cabbage Soup

Serves 4

This is an elaborate clear broth soup and, by itself, can be a meal. It requires a few steps of preparation, including wrapping and tying ingredients into small packages. The end result shows the cook's careful execution that is appreciated by all.

1 head napa or white cabbage

20 stems Chinese celery or garlic chives

3 tablespoons vegetable oil

3 tablespoons thinly sliced shallots

1 cup chopped shiitake mushrooms or other mushrooms of your choice

2 tablespoons Chinese cooking wine [*shu shang*] or sherry wine

1 cup diced soft tofu, in 1/8-inch cubes

2 tablespoons chopped Chinese celery

1 tablespoon light soy sauce

1 tablespoon Maggi Seasoning Sauce

1 tablespoon sugar

5 cups vegetable stock

1/4 cup dried lily buds, soaked in warm water (optional)

Salt

2 tablespoons chopped fresh cilantro leaves, for garnish

2 tablespoons chopped green onions, for garnish

Separate the cabbage into individual leaves (about 20) to use as wrappers. Trim and discard the tough center ridges. Wash the leaves and set aside to drain. Trim and cut the Chinese celery stems or garlic chives into long, narrow strips for use as string ties.

Bring 5 cups of water to a boil in a medium saucepan. Add the cabbage leaves and celery stems and poach them until they are soft and pliable, about 2 minutes. Drain and rinse with cold water. Pat dry.

To make the stuffing, place the oil in a pan over medium heat. Add the shallots and sauté until light brown and fragrant. Stir in the mushrooms and cook for 2 minutes. Add the cooking wine and stir to mix well. Stir in the tofu, chopped celery, soy sauce, Maggi Seasoning Sauce, and sugar. Cook until heated through, about 3 minutes. Remove from the heat.

Spread the cabbage leaves and place about 2 tablespoons of the stuffing on each leaf. Fold in the edges and shape into square packages. Tie and secure the packages with the celery strings in preparation for cooking.

Place the stock in a medium saucepan and bring to a boil over medium heat. Drain the optional lily buds and add them to the stock. Add the wrapped tofu packages and simmer for 3 minutes or until they are heated through. Adjust the flavor with salt and other seasonings to taste.

Transfer to individual bowls and garnish with the chopped cilantro and green onions before serving.

Sour Curry Soup

Serves 6

Gaeng Som

This dish is a curry soup made with a light, spicy broth and sweet-and-sour tamarind liquid, without any coconut products. It is a refreshing change from the rich, creamy, heavily coconut-based curries. If you don't like cauliflower, try napa cabbage, long beans, or swamp cabbage as delicious substitutes.

4 cups vegetable stock

$\frac{1}{3}$ cup Sour Curry Paste *Gaeng Som*, page 51, or 3 tablespoons ready-made paste

2 cups sliced mushrooms of your choice, in bite-size pieces

1 cup cauliflower florets or chopped napa cabbage

1 cup sliced long beans or green beans, in 1 $\frac{1}{2}$-inch lengths

$\frac{1}{2}$ cup tamarind liquid

3 tablespoons light soy sauce, or more to taste

2 tablespoons sugar, or more to taste

Fresh lime juice

Place the stock in a medium saucepan over medium heat and bring to a boil. Stir in the curry paste. Add the mushrooms, cauliflower, long beans, tamarind liquid, soy sauce, and sugar. Simmer for 3–5 minutes or until the vegetables are tender. Adjust the flavor by adding lime juice and more soy sauce and sugar to taste. Serve hot with steamed rice.

Sweet Five-Spice Soup

Tom Palo

Serves 6

This slow cooked, stew-like soup borrows five-spice from Chinese cuisine and then adds a touch of other flavorings to suit the Thai sweet palate. It should be cooked in advance so the flavors can marry and deepen.

Soak the dried mushrooms in warm water for 15 minutes or until fully expanded. Squeeze lightly to drain the water and discard any tough stems.

Combine the mushrooms and the remaining ingredients in a large pot and place over medium-low heat. Simmer for 30 minutes or until the vegetables are tender. Discard the cinnamon sticks and star anise before serving. Serve with steamed rice.

4 cups dried black mushrooms (about 1 pound)

8 cups vegetable stock or water

5 cups fried (one-square-inch pieces) spongy tofu (1 1/2–2 pounds)

3 cups diced daikon, in 1/2-inch cubes (about 1 pound)

1/3 cup brown sugar, or more to taste

1/4 cup chopped shallots

3 tablespoons Chinese five-spice powder

3 tablespoons chopped garlic

3 tablespoons chopped fresh cilantro roots or stems

3 tablespoons light soy sauce

3 tablespoons sweet soy sauce

2 tablespoons Maggi Seasoning Sauce

1 tablespoon whole black peppercorns

1 tablespoon vegetable base, or 1 vegetable bouillon cube

2 sticks cinnamon

3 whole star anise

Salt

Vegetable Peppery Broth

Serves 6

Thai soup can be hot without using any chilies. The hotness comes from black peppercorns, which impart a peppery, spicy heat rather than the fiery heat from chilies. Thai or Asian black peppercorns are spicier than their Western counterpart. Adjust the amount of peppercorns according to their origin to fit your preference. Lemon basil [bai mangluk[is essential for adding an aromatic final touch, as it harmonizes all the flavors.

SPICE PASTE:

2 teaspoons whole black peppercorns, or more to taste

1/2 cup chopped shallots

I tablespoon fermented bean curds (optional)

VEGETABLES:

5 cups vegetable stock

2 cups sliced mushrooms of your choice

I cup peeled and diced kabocha squash or pumpkin, in 1/4-inch cubes

I cup diced Asian bottle gourds or zucchini, in 1/4-inch cubes

I cup diced baby corn, in 1/4-inch cubes

I cup sliced long beans, in I-inch lengths

3 tablespoons light soy sauce, or more to taste

I tablespoon sugar, or more to taste

I tablespoon vegetable base, or I vegetable bouillon cube

I cup lemon basil leaves [*bai mangluk*]

Combine all the paste ingredients in a mortar with pestle and pound until the mixture forms a smooth paste. Alternatively, combine all the ingredients in a food processor and process into a smooth paste.

Place the stock in a medium saucepan and bring to a boil over medium heat. Stir in the spice paste. Add the mushrooms, squash, bottle gourds, baby corn, and long beans, and simmer for 5–7 minutes or until the vegetables are almost tender.

Stir in the soy sauce, sugar, and vegetable base. Simmer for 3–5 minutes or until the vegetables are fully tender. Adjust the flavor by adding more seasonings to taste and remove from the heat. Sprinkle with the lemon basil leaves and serve immediately with steamed rice.

Stir-fries

Chinese cuisine has had a tremendous influence on the way Thais cook and eat. Ingredients such as noodles have followed the long-established trade routes between the two countries, and Chinese noodle recipes have been incorporated into the Thai repertoire. Wok and stir-fry techniques have been of utmost importance in Thai kitchens. The most popular Thai noodle dish, pad thai, is a variation of the Chinese stir-fry, with local Thai ingredients and seasonings added to suit the Thai palate.

Like its Chinese counterpart, Thai stir-fry also requires intense heat in order for the food to cook quickly. Staging is important: each ingredient must be prepared before the actual cooking begins. Preparation of the ingredients takes time—chopping, slicing, dicing, and apportioning—but the actual cooking time is usually less than ten minutes. Stir-fry dishes must be removed from the wok piping hot and served immediately to maintain the crisp freshness of the ingredients. Most Thai dishes are cooked in woks because of their convenience and ability to cook foods rapidly.

To start stir-frying, first heat the wok. Then add a little vegetable oil and heat it almost to the smoking point. Cook the spices (mainly garlic and shallots) first until they are light brown; this will bring out their full fragrance. This usually does not take very long in the hot oil. Then add the other ingredients and seasonings—starting with the longer-cooking items, such as carrots, and ending with the quick-cooking items, such as bean sprouts—and stir until they are evenly mixed. Controlling the amount of liquid in the stir-fry is critical, since high heat will cause the moisture to evaporate quickly and could result in a burned, bitter, dry, salty stir-fry. If there is too much liquid, it will no longer be a stir-fry but rather a poached or boiled dish, and it will lack the sheen from a flavorful sauce. Adding the right amount of liquid at the appropriate time will enhance both the flavor and texture of the dish. Novice stir-fryers often overcook their food; getting just the right timing takes practice. Tasting the food is the easiest way to tell whether it is ready or not. Cook the vegetables just to al dente, as they will continue to cook to perfection in a serving plate as it is being brought to the table.

In addition to stir-frying, a wok is used for steaming (with a bamboo steamer set), deep-frying, and smoking. It can also be used as a pot, a floating device during a flood, and sometimes as a saucer for snow-sledding.

Fried Tofu with Sweet-and-Sour Chilies

Serves 6

Tao Hu Sam Ros

Crispy and crunchy are as important to the texture of this dish as sweet and sour are to the flavor. Many easy cooking steps are used, and all the ingredients can be prepared ahead of time. A final assembly is needed just before serving to ensure the crispy, crunchy texture that is enhanced by the unique sweet-and-sour flavors of the tamarind sauce.

2 pounds firm tofu, drained well

½ teaspoon salt

3 cups vegetable oil, for deep-frying

1 cup sweet basil leaves [*bai horapha*], patted completely dry

3 tablespoons thinly sliced garlic

3 tablespoons thinly sliced shallots

½ cup chopped fresh chilies (jalapeño or serrano)

¼ cup chopped garlic

¼ cup chopped shallots

¼ cup chopped fresh cilantro roots or stems

2 tablespoons chopped fresh Thai chilies (optional, for more heat)

¼ cup palm sugar, or more to taste

¼ cup tamarind liquid, or more to taste

2 tablespoons light soy sauce, or more to taste

1 tablespoon vegetable base, or 1 vegetable bouillon cube

2 tablespoons fresh lime juice, or more to taste

Cut the tofu into ½ x ½ x 2-inch strips. Sprinkle with the salt, and set aside.

Heat the oil in a wok or deep pan over medium heat. When hot, add the sweet basil leaves, sliced garlic, and sliced shallots, one at a time; fry 2–3 minutes for the basil leaves and 3–5 minutes for the garlic and shallots or until light brown and crispy. Do not burn. Strain and remove from the hot oil, and drain on absorbent paper or paper towels. Set aside for the topping.

With the same oil, fry the tofu for 5–7 minutes or until golden brown and crispy on all sides. Remove and drain on absorbent paper or paper towels.

Combine the fresh chilies, chopped garlic, shallots, cilantro roots, and optional Thai chilies in a mortar with pestle or in a food processor. Grind until the mixture is well blended. Do not overprocess into a paste.

Heat 3 tablespoons of the oil in a saucepan over medium heat and cook the ground herb mixture 3–5 minutes or until light brown and fragrant. Add the sugar, tamarind liquid, soy sauce, and vegetable base. Continue cooking for 5–7 minutes or until the sugar is dissolved and the sauce turns syrupy. Adjust the flavor with lime juice and more soy sauce and sugar to taste.

To serve, arrange the fried tofu on a serving platter and top with the sauce. Sprinkle with the crispy fried basil, garlic, and shallots.

Fried Rice

Serves 4

Leftover rice is the most suitable starch for this dish, as its dry texture won't become mushy when fried. If using fresh steamed rice, spread the rice on a tray and refrigerate it for thirty minutes to make it drier. Because this is a stir-fry dish, which takes just a few minutes to cook, all the ingredients should be prepared in advance.

3 tablespoons vegetable oil

2 tablespoons minced garlic

1 cup diced firm tofu, in $1/4$-inch cubes

1 cup diced carrots, in $1/8$-inch cubes

1 cup long beans or green beans, thinly sliced crosswise

$1/2$ cup diced onions, in $1/8$-inch cubes

2 cups steamed rice, crumbled into individual grains

2 tablespoons light soy sauce, or more to taste

2 tablespoons sugar, or more to taste

1 tablespoon Maggi Seasoning Sauce

$1/4$ cup sliced green onions, in 1-inch lengths

$1/4$ cup julienne red bell peppers

$1/2$ teaspoon pepper

1 cup sliced English cucumbers, in half circles

1 lime, cut into 4 wedges

Heat the oil in a wok or skillet over medium heat. When the oil is hot, add the garlic and stir-fry for 2 minutes or until it is light brown and fragrant. Stir in the tofu and mix well.

Increase the heat to high and add the diced carrots, long beans, and onions. Cook and stir for 3–5 minutes or until the vegetables are almost crisp-tender.

Add the steamed rice, soy sauce, sugar, and Maggi Seasoning Sauce. Stir to mix well, and cook for 3 minutes or until heated through. Adjust the flavor with more seasonings to taste. Stir in the green onions and bell peppers before removing from the heat.

Transfer to a serving platter and sprinkle with the pepper. Serve with the cucumber and lime wedges on the side.

Stir-fried Flambé Morning Glory

Serves 6

Puk Bung Fai Daeng

This dish creates a spectacle, drawing a crowd much like a flame throwing. The wok and oil are subject to extreme heat and a high flame until they are smoking. Drenched morning glory is quickly added and when water meets hot oil, sparks fly.

1 1/2 pounds morning glory or Chinese broccoli [*gai lan*] or spinach
3 tablespoons chopped garlic
2 tablespoons fermented yellow bean sauce or fermented black beans
1 tablespoon chopped fresh Thai chilies (optional)
1 tablespoon light soy sauce
1 tablespoon sugar (optional)
2 tablespoons water
3 tablespoons vegetable oil

Wash the morning glory and trim off the tough stems. Cut into 2-inch lengths and place on a big plate. Top the morning glory with the garlic, fermented yellow bean sauce, optional Thai chilies, soy sauce, optional sugar, and water.

Heat the oil in a wok over high heat until smoking. Turn over the morning glory plate and quickly dump all ingredients into the hot oil. Be careful when the water meets the hot oil and sparks the flambé.

Shake the wok a few times to toss the mixture or stir to mix well. Cook 2–3 minutes or until heated through. Transfer to a serving plate and serve immediately.

Glass Noodles in a Clay Pot

Serves 6

In this dish, noodles are steamed slowly in the juice from vegetables. Cooking in a clay pot lends an earthy and smoky aroma as smoke and heat are filtered through the fine clay. Glass or cellophane noodles are made from mung beans and are a good source of protein in the vegetarian diet.

S oak the noodles, dried mushrooms, and optional lily buds separately in warm water for 10–15 minutes or until they are soft and fully expanded. Strain and squeeze lightly to dry. Cut the noodles into 6-inch strands and thinly slice the mushrooms.

Combine the vegetable stock, ginger, cornstarch, chopped garlic, soy sauce, stir-fry sauce, sugar, Maggi Seasoning Sauce, pepper, and sesame oil in a small bowl. Stir to mix well.

Place the vegetable oil in a nine-inch clay pot or regular saucepan with a tight-fitting lid and place over medium heat. Stir in the mushrooms, lily buds, diced carrots, baby corn, and peas. Cook

3 ounces dried cellophane or glass noodles [*woon sen*]

1 cup dried black mushrooms

¼ cup dried lily buds (optional)

½ cup vegetable stock or water

¼ cup julienne fresh young ginger

2 tablespoons cornstarch

2 tablespoons chopped garlic

2 tablespoons light soy sauce

2 tablespoons vegetarian or mushroom stir-fry sauce

1 tablespoon sugar

1 tablespoon Maggi Seasoning Sauce

1 teaspoon pepper

1 teaspoon sesame oil

2 tablespoons vegetable oil

1 cup diced carrots, in ¼-inch cubes

1 cup diced baby corn, in bite-size pieces

½ cup frozen green peas

2 cups diced firm silken tofu, in ½-inch cubes

½ cup sliced green onions, in 1-inch lengths, for garnish

and stir to mix well. Add the noodles and tofu. Stir gently and fold to combine well.

Stir the vegetable stock mixture and then add it to the pot. Stir gently and fold to mix well. Reduce the heat to low and cover with the lid. Continue cooking for 15–20 minutes or until the vegetables are cooked and the noodles have absorbed all the liquid.

Garnish with the green onions and serve in the clay pot or transfer to a serving platter and garnish.

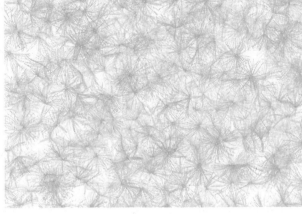

Stir-fried Assorted Vegetables

Serves 6

This is the ultimate vegetable stir-fry; it has a wide variety of Asian vegetables, and they infuse all sorts of flavors and textures. Vegetables of your choice can be used as long as their cooking times have been taken into consideration. Preparing the vegetables in particular sizes (for instance, slicing or dicing longer-cooking carrots so that the pieces are smaller than quick-cooking mushrooms) will help ensure that everything will be cooked evenly.

1/2 cup vegetable stock or water

3 tablespoons vegetarian or mushroom stir-fry sauce

3 tablespoons sugar, or more to taste

2 tablespoons light soy sauce, or more to taste

2 tablespoons rice vinegar

2 tablespoons cornstarch

1 tablespoon vegetable base, or 1 vegetable bouillon cube

1 tablespoon fermented yellow bean sauce or fermented black beans

3 tablespoons vegetable oil

3 tablespoons minced garlic

2 tablespoons minced fresh ginger

1 cup sliced baby bok choy, in bite-site pieces

1 cup sliced Chinese broccoli [*gai lan*], in bite-site pieces (optional)

1 cup sliced long beans or green beans, in 1 1/2-inch lengths

1 cup thinly sliced Asian long eggplant (optional)

1 cup diced water chestnuts, in 1/4-inch cubes (optional)

1 cup sliced napa cabbage, in bite-size pieces

1 cup julienne colored bell peppers (red, orange, or yellow)

1/2 cup diced onions, in 1/4-inch cubes

1/2 cup sliced green onions, in 1-inch lengths

5 sprigs fresh cilantro, for garnish

Combine the vegetable stock, stir-fry sauce, sugar, light soy sauce, vinegar, cornstarch, vegetable base, and fermented bean sauce in a small bowl. Stir to mix well. Set aside.

Heat the oil in a wok or skillet over high heat. Add the garlic and ginger and sauté 2–3 minutes or until light brown and fragrant. Add the bok choy, optional broccoli, long beans, optional eggplant, water chestnuts, napa cabbage, bell peppers, and diced onions, and stir to mix well. Cook and stir 5–7 minutes.

Stir the vegetable stock mixture and add it to the wok. Stir and cook 3–5 minutes or until the sauce thickens and is heated through. The sauce should be thick enough to coat the vegetables. Add more water if needed. Adjust the flavor with more seasonings to taste.

Continue cooking until the vegetables are tender. Add the green onions before removing from the heat. Transfer to a serving platter and garnish with the cilantro.

Stir-fried Cashew Nuts

Serves 6

Cashew is a fruit tree and considered a type of mango in Thailand. A single cashew nut, which dangles underneath its fruit, is the seed; it develops in this unusual manner outside the fruit.

Cashew nuts are an essential commodity of South Thailand, where they grow commercially. They are a superb ingredient in many dishes and are valued for their unique flavor and texture. This dish calls for mild-flavored tofu or mushrooms to complement the crunchy texture and nutty taste of the cashews. This combination of tofu or mushrooms with cashew nuts is one of the best Thai vegetarian stir-fry dishes.

3 tablespoons vegetable oil

6 whole dried Thai chilies

2 tablespoons minced garlic

3 cups sliced mushrooms of your choice

1 cup sliced firm tofu, in 1/4-inch cubes

1 cup sliced onions

1 cup julienne colored bell peppers (red, orange, or yellow)

2 tablespoons vegetarian or mushroom stir-fry sauce

1 tablespoon light soy sauce, or more to taste

1 tablespoon sugar, or more to taste

1 tablespoon vegetable base, or 1 vegetable bouillon cube

1 cup roasted cashew nuts

1/2 cup sliced green onions, in 1-inch lengths, for garnish

3 sprigs fresh cilantro, leaves only, for garnish

Heat the oil in a wok over high heat. Add the dried chilies and fry them for 1–2 minutes or until they are crispy. Remove from the wok and set aside to drain on absorbent paper or paper towels.

Add the garlic to the wok and cook for 2–3 minutes or until fragrant. Stir in the mushrooms, tofu, onions, and bell peppers; stir-fry 3–5 minutes or until the vegetables are almost tender.

Add the stir-fry sauce, soy sauce, sugar, and vegetable base and stir to mix well. Continue stir-frying until all the vegetables are tender, about 3 minutes longer. Add the cashew nuts, green onions, and fried chilies. Continue cooking until heated through, about 2 minutes longer. Transfer to a serving platter and garnish with the cilantro before serving.

Stir-fried Red Curry Green Beans

Serves 6

Pad Prik King

This is a simple stir-fry dish with a twist of added curry paste. Again the simple, uncomplicated red curry paste [namprik gaeng koa] is used just enough to complement the green beans.

3 fresh kaffir lime leaves

2 tablespoons vegetable oil

1/4 cup Gaeng Koa Curry Paste, page 43, or 3 tablespoons ready-made paste

1 cup julienne firm tofu

3 cups sliced green beans or long beans, in 1 1/2-inch lengths

1 cup vegetable stock or water

2 tablespoons sugar, or more to taste

2 tablespoons light soy sauce, or more to taste

2 tablespoons chili paste with soybean oil [*namprik pow*]

1 tablespoon vegetable base, or 1 vegetable bouillon cube

2 whole red jalapeño peppers, sliced into thin strips, for garnish

5 sprigs Thai sweet basil [*bai horapha*], leaves only, for garnish

Stack the kaffir lime leaves and roll them tightly into a cigarette-like roll. Slice across the roll to make fine, paper-thin strips. Set aside for garnish.

Heat the oil in a wok or skillet over medium heat. Stir in the curry paste and cook 3–5 minutes or until fragrant. Add the tofu and cook and stir about 2 minutes.

Increase the heat to high and add the green beans. Stir-fry 3–5 minutes or until almost tender. Add the vegetable stock, sugar, soy sauce, chili paste with soybean oil, and vegetable base. Continue cooking until the beans are tender, about 3 minutes longer. Adjust the flavor with more seasonings to taste.

Transfer to a serving plate and garnish with the kaffir lime leaves, red jalapeño peppers, and basil leaves.

Stir-fried Eggplant with Holy Basil

Serves 6

Pad Kaprow

In the Thai kitchen, three kinds of basil are often used: sweet, lemon, and holy basil. Each has unique characteristics suitable for enhancing and pairing tastes in selected dishes.

Holy basil [bai kaprow] gives this dish authenticity and a snappy, spicy aftertaste. Holy basil is hard to find in the United States, except in midsummer when it thrives. Other basils can be substituted, but first try the authentic version. There is a holy difference.

¼ cup vegetable oil, or more as needed

1 bunch (2 cups) holy basil leaves [*bai kaprow*], patted dry

¼ cup thinly sliced shallots, for garnish

3 tablespoons minced garlic

3 tablespoons minced shallots

3 tablespoons minced fresh Thai chilies or jalapeños, more or less to taste

2 cups thinly sliced Asian eggplants, cut into rounds

1 cup sliced long beans or green beans, in 1 ½-inch lengths

1 cup julienne red bell peppers

3 tablespoons light soy sauce

3 tablespoons vegetarian or mushroom stir-fry sauce

2 tablespoons sugar

2 tablespoons rice vinegar

1 tablespoon vegetable base, or 1 vegetable bouillon cube

Heat the oil in a wok or deep skillet over medium heat. Fry half of the basil leaves until crispy but not burned, about 3 minutes. Remove from the oil and drain on absorbent paper or paper towels. Set aside for garnish. With the same oil, fry the sliced shallots until light brown and crispy, about 3 minutes. Remove from the oil and drain on absorbent paper or paper towels; set aside for garnish.

In the same wok or skillet, heat a little oil over high heat. Add the minced garlic, minced shallots, and chilies, and sauté 2–3 minutes or until fragrant. Add the eggplants and stir-fry 3–5 minutes or until almost tender.

Add the long beans and bell peppers. Mix well and stir-fry about 3 minutes. Stir in the soy sauce, stir-fry sauce, sugar, vinegar, and vegetable base. Continue stir-frying until the vegetables are tender, about 3 minutes longer. Add a little water if the mixture seems too dry.

Before removing from the heat, stir in the remaining fresh basil leaves and mix well. Transfer to a serving platter and garnish with the fried basil and shallots.

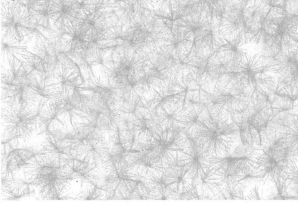

Stir-fried Stuffed Steamed Eggplants

Serves 6

Steaming is perhaps an uncommon way to prepare egg-plant. This dish offers an unusual paring of eggplant's unique soft texture and flavor combined with a sweet-and-sour filling. It is distinctive in texture, flavor, and appearance.

Steam the whole eggplants, stems attached, in a steamer over boiling water for 10–15 minutes or until tender and the skins wrinkle and turn brownish. Remove from the heat and let cool. Peel and discard the skins. Cut a long, length-wise slit in the middle of each eggplant to create a deep pocket; do not cut all the way through the eggplant. Set aside and keep warm for stuffing.

Heat the oil in a wok or skillet over medium heat. When hot, add the sliced shallots and fry 2–3 minutes or until light brown and crispy. Remove from the oil and drain on absorbent paper or paper towels. Set aside for garnish. With the same oil, fry the 1 cup of basil leaves for 2–3 minutes or until dark green and crispy. Set aside for garnish.

6 whole Asian long eggplants, purple or green
1/4 cup vegetable oil, or more as needed
1/4 cup thinly sliced shallots, for garnish
1 cup Thai sweet basil leaves [*bai horapha*], for garnish
2 tablespoons minced garlic
2 tablespoons minced fresh cilantro roots or stems
2 tablespoons minced shallots
2 cups finely chopped firm tofu
3 tablespoons light soy sauce
2 tablespoons sugar
2 tablespoons tamarind liquid or rice vinegar
1 tablespoon vegetable base, or 1 vegetable bouillon cube
1 tablespoon red chili sauce [*sambal olek*] (optional)
1/2 cup chopped Thai sweet basil leaves [*bai horapha*]
1/2 cup diced colored bell peppers (red, orange, or yellow), in 1/8-inch cubes, for garnish

In the same wok, add the minced garlic, cilantro roots, and minced shallots. Stir-fry 2–3 minutes or until fragrant. Add the tofu, soy sauce, sugar, tamarind liquid, vegetable base, and optional red chili sauce, and stir to mix well. Continue to stir-fry for 2–3 minutes. If the mixture seems too dry, add a little water. Adjust the flavor by adding more soy sauce and sugar to taste. Stir in the ½ cup chopped fresh basil leaves and remove from the heat.

To serve, heat the eggplants in a microwave for 2–3 minutes and then stuff them with the tofu mixture, mounding it high. Garnish with the fried shallots, fried basil leaves, and diced bell peppers before serving.

Stir-fried Tofu with Basil

Serves 6

This is another version of stir-fry using holy basil, one of three popular basils in Thai cooking, to enhance the dish with its aroma. It is considered a hot-and-spicy dish with a lot of Thai chilies and snappy, spicy holy basil. The dish was dubbed with the name kee mow, *meaning "drunkard," as its strong flavor can jolt and awaken the taste buds of even the heaviest drinkers.*

1/4 cup vegetable oil, or more as needed

1 bunch holy basil [*bai kaprow*], leaves only (about 2 cups)

2 cups julienne firm tofu

1/4 cup finely minced shallots

3 tablespoons finely minced garlic

3 tablespoons finely minced fresh Thai chilies, more or less to taste

2 cups sliced long beans or green beans, in 1 1/2-inch lengths

2 tablespoons sugar, or more to taste

2 tablespoons light soy sauce

2 tablespoons vegetarian or mushroom stir-fry sauce

1 tablespoon vegetable base, or 1 vegetable bouillon cube

1 cup roasted cashews

1/2 cup julienne colored bell peppers (red, orange, or yellow), for garnish

Heat the oil in a wok or skillet over medium heat. When hot, add half of the basil leaves (reserve the other half) and fry 2–4 minutes or until crispy. Remove from the oil and drain on absorbent paper or paper towels. Set aside for garnish.

With the same oil, fry the julienne tofu for 3–5 minutes or until light brown. Remove from the pan and drain on absorbent paper or paper towels.

Heat a little oil in the same wok over high heat. Stir in the shallots, garlic, and chilies. Cook 3–5 minutes or until fragrant. Add the tofu, long beans, sugar, light soy sauce, stir-fry sauce, and vegetable base. Stir fry 3–5 minutes longer until well mixed.

Stir in the remaining fresh basil leaves and the roasted cashews. Transfer to a serving platter and garnish with the bell peppers and fried basil leaves.

Stir-fried Thai Noodles

When Thai cuisine is the subject of conversation in social circles, pad thai is often the place where it all starts and ends. Each chef has a signature version of this quintessential Thai dish, differing in ingredients, techniques, and leading flavors. In the United States, every Thai restaurant has pad thai on the menu, and it's usually the top selling dish. In Thailand, you'll find street vendors and restaurants offering pad thai on every corner, something akin to the American burger stand. Why is this dish so popular? Maybe it's the three distinct flavors of sweet, sour, and salty mingling within each bite. Maybe it's the zesty hint of spiciness capped with a crunchy texture and nutty taste from roasted peanuts. Maybe it's the "comfort food" nature of noodles. The popularity of this dish will undoubtedly drive chefs and diners alike to continue their search for the ultimate pad thai.

Pad thai dates back to seventeenth century Thailand when Siam began trading with China. The Chinese arrived with noodles, woks, and the new technique of stir-frying. Chinese chefs became employed in the Thai court, adding more variety to the royal kitchen. Chinese immigrants established an ethnic community and soon one of their noodle dishes became popular among Thai people. The dish was called "pad chinese," or Chinese stir-fry noodles. It consisted of medium-size rice noodles, soy sauce, garlic chives, bean sprouts, preserved turnips, dried shrimp, sugar, and distilled vinegar. Using local ingredients to appeal to their palate, the Thai people modified the dish by replacing the soy sauce with fish sauce, the sugar with palm sugar, and the vinegar with tamarind liquid and lime juice. They added shrimp fat and chili powder or chili flakes for flavor and color. Other ingredients mostly remained the same. They named their dish "pad thai" to avoid confusion with the Chinese version. Another important distinction between these two dishes was the way they were served. Pad thai was served on a large plate with a fork and spoon, accompanied by fresh vegetables such as bean sprouts, banana flowers, and green onions, while pad chinese was served in a bowl with chopsticks and no side vegetables.

Cooking pad thai is quick and satisfying. As a stir-fry dish, pad thai takes just a few minutes of actual cooking. But the preparation of ingredients is the real task and must be done beforehand, making this a great dish for the social chef who likes to prepare ahead of the guests' arrival. Fresh and dried medium-size rice noodles are readily available. Fresh noodles are the best, but dried noodles called *chantaboon* are popular among Thais, as they come from the town of Chantaboon, which makes the best noodles for pad thai. The dried noodles are also easy to handle. The noodles should be soaked in warm water until pliable (al dente), but not fully soft. Then they can be cooked with ease in a wok without quickly fusing together and turning into a gluey ball of rice. The fresh noodles have a lot of moisture and require fast execution by an experienced cook to prevent them from becoming mushy. Chopping and mincing the ingredients—such as garlic, preserved turnips, and roasted peanuts—is another key to creating the ultimate pad thai.

Cooking pad thai requires constant attention and adjustment because the precise amount of heat and moisture contribute to the proper consistency of the noodles and the right combination of flavors. Too much moisture and not enough heat or overcooking will make the dish mushy. Not enough moisture and too much heat will make it tough and dry. If you're cooking pad thai for first time, be patient and enjoy your research. Start your pad thai by making a small portion, just enough for one person, which is what most Thai restaurants do. A small portion is easy to handle and can be heated evenly in the home kitchen without a commercial stir-fry (wok) stove. Your ultimate pad thai may be many tries away, but don't worry. Thai chefs make hundreds of attempts to perfect this dish.

Stir-fried Thai Noodles

Serves 6

Soak the rice noodles in warm water until soft and pliable (al dente), about 30 minutes. Check the water temperature occasionally. If it is no longer warm, refresh the water. Drain and set aside.

Heat a wok or large skillet on high heat. Add the oil. When hot, add the garlic and cook until fragrant, about 2 minutes. Add the mushrooms and stir-fry for 3 minutes. Add the soaked and drained noodles and stir until well coated with the oil.

Add the sugar, soy sauce, tamarind liquid, vinegar, and paprika (these ingredients may be combined in advance). Stir-fry the mixture until thoroughly combined and the liquid is absorbed. Stir in the tofu and preserved turnips. Check the noodle texture; it should be cooked and soft. Add some water if the noodles are too dry or too tough. If they fall apart easily, they are overcooked.

Pad Thai

7–8 ounces dried, medium rice noodles, chantaboon type

3 tablespoons vegetable oil

2 tablespoons minced garlic

3 cups sliced mushrooms of your choice

1/4 cup sugar, or more to taste

1/4 cup light soy sauce, or more to taste

2 tablespoons tamarind liquid

2 tablespoons distilled white vinegar, or more to taste

1 tablespoon paprika or chili powder

2 cups julienne fried tofu

3 tablespoons minced preserved turnips

3 cups bean sprouts, plus more for accompaniment

1/2 cup sliced garlic chives or green onions, in 1-inch lengths

1/3 cup chopped roasted peanuts

1/2 cup julienne red bell peppers, for garnish

5 sprigs fresh cilantro, leaves only, for garnish

1 whole lime, cut into 6 wedges, for accompaniment

Stir in the bean sprouts, garlic chives, and peanuts. Continue stir-frying until heated through and well combined. Adjust the flavor with more soy sauce, vinegar, and sugar to taste.

Transfer to individual plates and garnish with the red bell peppers and cilantro. Serve with fresh bean sprouts and the lime wedges on the side. For a refreshing lime flavor, diners may squeeze the lime juice over their pad thai.

This recipe is pictured on the cover.

Stir-fried Vermicelli Noodles

Serves 6

This is the perfect one-plate dish with the right proportion of protein from mung bean noodles and minerals from carrots, leeks, and spinach. It has its origins in Korean cuisine, as evidenced by the sesame products and native cooking techniques. Kim chee (a pungent Korean dish made of fermented pickled vegetables, such as cabbage or turnips) as an accompaniment is a sure sign of the foreign influence on this adapted Thai dish.

8 ounces dried mung bean glass noodles [*woon sen*] or rice vermicelli noodles [*sen mee*]

2 tablespoons light soy sauce, or more to taste

1 teaspoon sesame oil

2 tablespoons vegetable oil

2 tablespoons thinly sliced shallots

1 tablespoon dried chili flakes, or more to taste

2 cups julienne carrots

2 cups julienne leeks

2 cups thinly sliced shiitake mushrooms

1 tablespoon Maggi Seasoning Sauce, or more to taste

$1/2$ teaspoon pepper

$1/4$ pound baby spinach

2 tablespoons roasted sesame seeds, for garnish

1 cup spicy *kim chee*, as an accompaniment (optional)

Soak the noodles in warm water until soft and pliable (al dente), about 20 minutes. Check the water temperature occasionally. If it is no longer warm, refresh the water. Drain well in a colander and set aside.

Heat the soy sauce and sesame oil in a wok over medium heat. When hot, add the noodles. Stir-fry to mix well and heat through, about 3 minutes. Transfer to a bowl. Wipe the wok clean with towels.

Add the vegetable oil to the wok and increase the heat to high. Add the shallots and dried chili flakes. Stir-fry 1–2 minutes or until fragrant. Stir in the carrots and leeks and cook 2–3 minutes longer.

Stir in the mushrooms, Maggi Seasoning Sauce, and pepper. Continue cooking until the vegetables are tender, about 3 minutes longer. Return the noodles to the wok and toss to mix well. Adjust the flavor with more seasonings to taste. Remove from the heat.

To serve, line a platter with the baby spinach and top with the noodles. Garnish with the roasted sesame seeds, and serve with the optional *kim chee* as an accompaniment.

Stir-fried Vermicelli Coconut Noodles

Serves 6

Instead of stir-fried noodles with a light sauce, this dish uses coconut milk to make a sweet and creamy sauce. It is quite simple and any vegetable of your choice can be added. The original Thai version uses red food coloring to give a pink hue to the noodles. Optional tomato paste can be added to the noodles while they are cooking in order to obtain the desire red hue.

8 ounces dried vermicelli rice noodles [*sen mee*]

1 1/2 cups coconut cream

1/4 cup thinly sliced shallots

2 cups julienne firm tofu

2 tablespoons sugar

2 tablespoons fermented yellow bean sauce
   or soybean paste

2 tablespoons tamarind liquid or rice vinegar

1 tablespoon dried chili flakes (optional)

1 tablespoon light soy sauce, or more to taste

2 cups bean sprouts

1/4 cup sliced garlic chives or green onions,
   in 1 1/2-inch lengths

1/2 teaspoon pepper

1/4 cup julienne red jalapeño or bell peppers, for
   garnish

3 sprigs fresh cilantro, leaves only, for garnish

1 whole lime, cut into 6 wedges

Soak the noodles in warm water until soft and pliable (al dente), about 20 minutes. Check the water temperature occasionally. If it is no longer warm, refresh the water. Drain well in a colander and set aside.

Place the coconut cream in a wok over medium heat and bring to a boil. Add the shallots and cook for 3 minutes. Stir in the tofu, sugar, fermented yellow bean sauce, tamarind liquid, optional chili flakes, and light soy sauce. Continue cooking for 3 minutes longer. Remove half of the mixture and reserve for later use as a sauce.

Add the noodles to the wok and stir for 3–5 minutes or until the liquid has been absorbed. The noodles should be cooked and soft; add more sauce if needed. Stir in the bean sprouts and garlic chives and mix well.

Transfer to a serving platter and sprinkle with the reserved sauce and ground pepper. Garnish with the red peppers and cilantro leaves. Serve with the lime wedges. For a refreshing lime flavor, diners may squeeze lime juice over their coconut noodles.

Stir-fried Wide Noodles with Sweet Soy

Serves 6

If pad thai is the number one noodle dish, pad se-iew is the runner-up. Wide rice noodles are used for this stir-fry dish. Sweet dark soy sauce [se-iew wan], made from soy sauce and molasses, is the main seasoning and is essential to this dish's caramel-like flavor and color. Chinese broccoli [gai lan], with its leathery leaves, crunchy stems, and musky sweet-and-bitter flavor, adds such complex taste and texture to this simple dish.

1 pound fresh wide rice noodles [*sen yai*], or ¹/₂ pound dried wide rice noodles

3 cups sliced Chinese broccoli [*gai lan*] or broccoli florets (1–1 ¹/₂ pounds)

3 tablespoons vegetable oil, or more as needed

3 tablespoons minced garlic

3 tablespoons sweet dark soy sauce [*se-iew wan*], or more to taste

2 cups thinly sliced firm tofu (optional)

3 tablespoons light soy sauce

2 tablespoons sugar

2 tablespoons vegetarian or mushroom stir-fry sauce

1 tablespoon rice vinegar

¹/₂ teaspoon pepper

¹/₄ cup thinly sliced jalapeño peppers, for accompaniment

¹/₄ cup distilled white vinegar or rice vinegar, for accompaniment

Separate the fresh noodles into individual strands. If using dried noodles, cook in boiling water until soft and pliable (al dente). Drain in a colander and rinse with cold water. Set aside to completely drain the water.

Trim and peel tough skin of the broccoli stems and slice the stems into thin strips. Cut the leaves or florets into bite-size pieces and set aside separately from the stems.

Heat the oil in a wok or skillet over high heat. Add the garlic and cook for 2 minutes or until light brown and fragrant. Stir in the noodles and cook until well coated with the oil.

Add the sweet soy sauce and stir to mix well. Cook and stir 3–5 minutes, making sure that all the noodles are well coated and colored evenly. Remove from the wok and set aside.

In the same wok with a little oil, stir in the optional tofu and the broccoli stems and cook until the stems are almost tender, about 3 minutes. Add the broccoli leaves, light soy sauce, sugar, vegetarian stir-fry sauce, and rice vinegar. Stir-fry 3–5 minutes or until the broccoli is tender.

Return the noodles to the wok and stir-fry to mix well and heat through. Adjust the flavor by adding more soy sauce and sugar to taste.

Transfer to a serving platter and sprinkle with the ground pepper.

Combine the jalapeño peppers and vinegar in a small bowl. Serve as an accompaniment on the side. Sprinkle over the noodles for an extra sour-and-spicy taste.

Vegetable Clay Pot

Serves 6

The use of caramel sauce in this recipe can be traced back to French cooking, which has had a tremendous influence on the cuisine of the Vietnamese, who are neighbors of the Thai people. Thais use their round clay pots to cook this dish instead of the flat-bottomed Vietnamese or Chinese clay pots, which are better suited to the flat-top cooking ranges found in Western kitchens.

2 cups julienne firm tofu

2 tablespoons finely minced garlic

2 tablespoons finely minced fresh ginger

1 tablespoon rice vinegar

1 teaspoon pepper

3 tablespoons vegetable oil

2 cups julienne shiitake mushrooms or other mushrooms of your choice

2 cups sliced green beans or snow peas, in 1-inch lengths

2 cups julienne carrots

5 whole fresh Thai chilies, bruised (optional)

¾ cup Soy Sauce Caramel (recipe follows)

2 tablespoons chopped fresh cilantro leaves, for garnish

6 sprigs fresh Thai sweet basil [bai horapha], for accompaniment

6 sprigs fresh cilantro, for accompaniment

Combine the tofu, garlic, ginger, vinegar, and pepper in a bowl and let marinate for at least 15 minutes.

In an eight-inch diameter clay pot or a regular saucepan with a lid, heat the oil over medium heat until almost smoking. Stir in the marinated tofu mixture and cook 2–3 minutes or until the garlic is fragrant. Add the mushrooms, green beans, carrots, and optional chilies, and stir to combine well. The tofu and vegetable mixture should be mounded high in the clay pot.

Add the prepared Soy Sauce Caramel to the clay pot and stir, folding in the sauce until it is well combined. Close the lid and cook over medium-low heat for 5–7 minutes or until the vegetables are tender and the sauce is reduced to a thick syrup.

Remove from the heat and sprinkle with the chopped cilantro leaves. Serve in the clay pot with a side dish of jasmine rice and the sprigs of fresh Thai sweet basil and cilantro.

To make the Soy Sauce Caramel, combine all the ingredients in a small saucepan and place over low heat. Simmer for 15–20 minutes until the mixture is reduced and turns into a thick syrup. While cooking, the syrup will emit a very pungent odor, so use a well-ventilated area.

SOY SAUCE CARAMEL: *Makes about ¾ cup*

¾ cup sugar

⅓ cup soy sauce

2 tablespoons water

Wide Noodles with Gravy

Serves 6

Most Thai stir-fried noodles, such as pad thai, are quite dry. In contrast, this dish has a flavorful gravy, adding a smooth texture to your eating experience. The noodles and gravy are prepared separately; they are combined a few minutes before serving.

Separate the fresh noodles into long, individual strands. If using dried noodles, cook in boiling water until soft (al dente). Rinse with cold water and drain.

Heat a wok over medium heat. Add the oil and swirl to coat the wok's surface. Stir in the garlic and cook for 2–3 minutes or until light brown and fragrant. Add the noodles and stir to coat with the oil so they won't stick to the wok. Add the sweet dark soy sauce and cook and stir for 3–5 minutes or until the noodles are evenly brown and heated through. Transfer to a serving platter or distribute among individual plates.

NOODLES:

1 pound fresh wide rice noodles [*sen yai*], or ½ pound dried rice noodles

3 tablespoons vegetable oil, or more as needed

1 tablespoon minced garlic

¼ cup sweet dark soy sauce [*se-iew wan*], or more to taste

GRAVY:

2 tablespoons vegetable oil

2 tablespoons minced garlic

2 cups sliced Chinese broccoli [*gai lan*] or broccoli florets

1 cup sliced baby corn or water chestnuts, in bite-size pieces

1 cup sliced mushrooms, in bite-size pieces

1 cup julienne carrots

2 tablespoons sugar, or more to taste

2 tablespoons light soy sauce, or more to taste

1 tablespoon fermented yellow bean sauce or fermented black beans

1 tablespoon vegetable base, or 1 vegetable bouillon cube

4 cups vegetable stock or water

3 tablespoons cornstarch, or more as needed

2 tablespoons water

2 teaspoons white pepper

5 whole jalapeño peppers, thinly sliced

½ cup distilled white vinegar or rice vinegar

To make the gravy, heat the oil in a wok over high heat. Add the garlic and sauté 2 minutes or until light brown and fragrant. Stir in the broccoli, corn, mushrooms, and carrots, and cook for 3 minutes or until almost tender. Don't overcook the vegetables.

Add the sugar, soy sauce, fermented yellow bean sauce, and vegetable base, and stir to mix well. Stir in the vegetable stock and bring to a boil.

Dissolve the cornstarch in the 2 tablespoons of water, and mix thoroughly. Add to the wok and mix well. Continue cooking until the mixture turns into a thick gravy. Adjust the flavor with more seasonings to taste. Pour the gravy over the noodles, distributing it evenly, and sprinkle with the white pepper before serving.

Combine the jalapeño peppers and vinegar in a small bowl and serve as a condiment. Sprinkle over the noodles for an extra sour-and-spicy taste.

Sweet-and-Sour Vegetable Plate

Serves 6

This colorful and refreshing dish can sure please a dinner crowd of all ages. Even a fussy eater who doesn't care for spicy or curry dishes will enjoy it. Kids like the sweet-and-sour flavor and candy-like colors of the vegetables and sauce.

Combine the vegetable stock, sugar, vinegar, light soy sauce, vegetarian stir-fry sauce, tomato paste, optional chili sauce, and cornstarch in a bowl. Stir to mix well and set aside.

Place the oil in a wok or skillet over high heat. Add the garlic and sauté 1–2 minutes or until light brown and fragrant. Add the tofu, diced pineapple, bell peppers, water chestnuts, and onions. Stir and cook for 3–5 minutes or until the vegetables are almost tender.

Stir the stock mixture and add it to the wok. Stir and cook 2–3 minutes or until the sauce thickens and is heated through. The sauce should be thick enough to lightly coat the vegetables. Adjust the flavor with more seasonings to taste.

Stir in the optional roasted cashews and the green onions before removing from the heat. Transfer to a serving platter and garnish with the cilantro.

1/2 cup vegetable stock or water

3 tablespoons sugar, or more to taste

3 tablespoons rice vinegar

2 tablespoons light soy sauce, or more to taste

2 tablespoons vegetarian or mushroom stir-fry sauce

2 tablespoons tomato paste, for coloring

2 tablespoons chili sauce [*sambal olek*] or Sriracha sauce (optional)

2 tablespoons cornstarch

3 tablespoons vegetable oil

3 tablespoons minced garlic

2 cups diced fried tofu, in 1/2-inch cubes

1 1/2 cup diced pineapple, in 1/4-inch cubes

1 1/2 cup diced colored bell peppers (red, orange, or yellow), in 1/4-inch cubes

1 cup diced water chestnuts, in 1/4-inch cubes

1 cup diced onions, in 1/4-inch cubes

1 cup roasted cashews (optional)

1/2 cup sliced green onions, in 1 1/2-inch lengths

4 sprigs fresh cilantro, for garnish

Pineapple Coconut Noodles, page 76

Curries and Other Main Dishes

Due to India's proximity to and trade with Thailand, the Thais have adopted many of India's beliefs and practices. Various aspects of Indian Hinduism and Buddhism are incorporated into Thai milestone events and ceremonies. These include ceremonial processions; incantations; dates, times, and locations for rites that are believed to augur well; and especially the food that is served. Some Thais arise each morning and perform a ritual for which they may not even know the derivation, such as a daily prayer, dressing in specific colors, or leaving the house facing in the right direction.

In addition to embracing India's religious beliefs, Thais have also readily accepted its food, such as curry, and added its complexity to the rather simple and straightforward traditional way of Thai cooking. Indian methods of making curry, as well as using dried herbs and spices, have added new depth to Thai cooking. Thais didn't just copy recipes; they incorporated local ingredients and created more complex flavors with their curry pastes, bringing both Indian and Thai herbs and spices to a heightened level of sophistication.

Curry paste-making in Thai cuisine is an art in itself. Recipes and tools, such as the stone mortar *(krok)* and pestle *(saak)* for curry paste-making, are handed down from generation to generation. However, this art form is quickly disappearing from Thai culture, since the latest generation hardly bothers to make curry paste from scratch, and ready-made generic products are easily found in supermarkets. Curry paste made from scratch with fresh ingredients and no

Green Papaya Salad, page 57

preservatives, and the use of a mortar and pestle, will result in a much better, more carefully prepared curry dish and reflect the personality of the cook. Pounding and grinding the ingredients with a stone pestle in a mortar is the best way to break down the oils and bring out the true essence of the ingredients. The amount of each ingredient can be adjusted according to personal taste. For example, the paste can be hot, medium, or mild, depending on the amount of chilies the cook decides to use. Likewise, the amount of a specific herb or spice used can be altered according to the cook's preference. Pounding and grinding seem to be a time-consuming and monotonous process at first, but with practice, it becomes a quick, fun, and effective way to prepare curry paste.

Thai curries are distinctively different from Indian curries, although a combination of Indian spices and Thai ingredients make unique Thai curries. For example, dried Indian spices, such as coriander, cumin, and cardamom, combined with fresh Thai ingredients—such as Thai galangal and lemongrass instead of the ginger commonly found in an Indian curry, or Thai kaffir lime leaves instead of Indian bay leaves—yield a delicious, complex curry paste. Thais add different varieties and colors (such as red, green, and yellow) of both the large and small chilies to create a wide range of curry pastes. They also use the local shrimp paste to enhance the musky-flavored Thai curries. For our purposes, fermented bean curds can be a substitute for shrimp paste, either of which can be eliminated.

Thai curries may be prepared with or without coconut milk. For rich, creamy, sweet curries, coconut milk or cream can be used as a base for the hearty dish. Clear broths rather than broths with coconut milk will result in lighter fare, yet will still maintain the essence of the herbs and spices. To produce the most flavorful curry, the dried herbs and spices are often roasted before being ground into the curry paste (dry-roasted in a pan over a stove, or roasted in a preheated oven until fragrant). More important, the longer a curry paste is cooked (without it burning), the more intense will be its flavor and color.

Once these fundamental but important steps are taken, all curry dishes are produced the same way: heat the pot, add liquids such as coconut milk or broths, add the vegetables, and adjust the taste with seasonings. Certain Thai curries taste better the second day, as resting and reheating them intensifies and harmonizes the flavors.

All Thai dishes—appetizers, soups, salads, and main dishes, except desserts— are served at the same time and can be eaten in any order. At least one kind of curry is usually a part of the Thai meal. Although most Thai dishes can hold their own in terms of bold taste, curries are often considered a main dish because of their rich, powerful flavors. A menu containing a curry must be carefully planned: the curry should complement, not overwhelm, the delicate flavors of the accompanying soup, salad, and stir-fry. A curry served over hot steamed rice can be a quick, one-dish meal, as the curry can be cooked a few days in advance and just reheated and poured over the rice. Many curries are equally popular over *kanom jeen* noodles accompanied by a medley of fresh and cooked vegetables.

Baked Mushroom and Asparagus

Serves 4

This oven-baked dish is easy to make using fresh, local, seasonal ingredients. To give depth to an otherwise rather plain dish, curry powder is added. It can be as spicy or mild as you like, depending on the type of curry powder used. There are generally three types: hot Madras, medium standard, and mild Chinese curry powder.

16 whole asparagus spears

1 cup diced water chestnuts, in ¼-inch cubes

1 cup diced firm tofu, in ¼-inch cubes (optional)

1 cup julienne sweet or colored bell peppers (red, orange, or yellow)

8 whole shiitake mushroom caps, stems removed

2 tablespoons curry powder of your choice

2 tablespoons light soy sauce

2 tablespoons sesame oil

1 tablespoon sugar

1 tablespoon rice vinegar

1 tablespoon vegetable base, or 1 vegetable bouillon cube, diluted with 2 tablespoons hot water

2 tablespoons thinly sliced red jalapeño or bell peppers, for garnish

3 sprigs fresh cilantro, for garnish

Trim the asparagus and poach in boiling water for 2–3 minutes or until almost tender. Remove from the hot water and rinse with cold water to stop further cooking. Drain and set aside. If using fresh water chestnuts, peel and poach them in boiling water for 2–3 minutes or until tender. Drain and set aside.

Preheat the oven to 350°F.

Combine all the ingredients, except the garnishes, in an ovenproof casserole dish with a lid or in a clay pot. Stir and fold to mix thoroughly. Bake for 15–20 minutes or until everything is tender and hot.

Remove from the oven and arrange on a serving platter or serve directly from the clay pot. Garnish with the red peppers and cilantro.

Coconut Rice

Serves 6

Rice is a staple in Thai cuisine and it accompanies almost every savory dish as a starch to help absorb intense flavors. There are many types of rice and many ways to cook it according to the meals, occasions, and different regions in the Thai kingdom. This dish is an attempt to break the monotony of eating plain steamed rice. It goes well with sweet curry dishes, such as Panaeng Curry, page 146, and hot and sour salads, such as Green Papaya Salad, page 57.

2 cups long-grain aromatic rice (Thai jasmine or Indian basmati)

2 cups vegetable stock, or 1 tablespoon vegetable base, or 1 vegetable bouillon cube combined with 2 cups water

1 1/2 cups coconut milk

2 tablespoons sugar (optional)

1 teaspoon salt

If using a rice cooker, combine all the ingredients and stir to mix well. Press the "on" switch and let the rice cook undisturbed for 45 minutes. Fluff the rice before serving.

If using a saucepan, combine all the ingredients and bring to a boil over medium-high heat. Reduce the heat to medium-low and cover with a lid. Cook the rice undisturbed for 10–15 minutes until fully cooked and all the liquid is absorbed. Turn off the heat and let stand on the still hot range for 10 minutes longer. Fluff the rice before serving.

Curried Coconut Noodles

Serves 4

This dish of noodles with coconut curry sauce is popular everywhere in Thailand. It is served as a one-plate dish and also a light meal, making a pleasant change from just eating plain rice. An array of fresh and cooked vegetables is essential as an accompaniment. Each region of Thailand—North, Northeast, Central, and South—has its own signature version, depending on local ingredients and palates.

SPICE PASTE:

5–8 large dried red chilies (California, New Mexico, or guajillo chilies)

1 cup minced lesser ginger [*kra-chai*]

3 tablespoons minced shallots

2 tablespoons minced lemongrass, tender midsection only

2 tablespoons minced garlic

1 tablespoon minced galangal

2 teaspoons fermented bean curds (optional)

1 teaspoon salt

Stem and seed the dried chilies. Soak them in warm water for 10–15 minutes or until soft. Drain and squeeze dry.

Using a mortar and pestle, pound and grind all the paste ingredients, starting with the chilies and adding one ingredient at a time until the mixture forms a smooth paste. Alternatively, combine all of the ingredients in a food processor and process into a smooth paste, adding a small amount of water to facilitate blending.

Bring 5 cups of water to a boil in a medium saucepan. Add the noodles and cook 5–7 minutes or until soft. Drain, rinse with cold water, and drain again. Portion the noodles into 3-ounce small wads, each about the size of a small bird's nest, and set aside.

In the same saucepan, bring 4 cups of water to a boil. Separately boil the long beans and then the morning glory for 3–5 minutes each or until tender.

Drain and set aside separately. Bring another 4 cups of water to a boil and add half of the bean sprouts (1½ cups). Boil for 1–2 minutes or until tender. Drain and set aside with the other half of fresh bean sprouts.

Arrange all the accompaniments on a serving platter.

Bring the vegetable stock to a boil in a medium saucepan over medium heat. Add the spice paste. Cook and stir the paste until it is completely dissolved. Crumble the tofu and add it to the saucepan. Cook and stir the tofu, breaking it down and stirring it well to get a smooth mixture. Stir in the coconut milk, soy sauce, and salt, and bring the mixture to a boil. Stir in the coconut cream and remove from the heat.

NOODLES, SAUCE, AND CONDIMENTS:

1 pound dried *kanom jeen* noodles or Japanese somen noodles

1 cup sliced long beans or green beans, in 1-inch lengths, as accompaniment

1 cup sliced morning glory, in 1-inch lengths, as accompaniment

3 cups fresh bean sprouts, as accompaniment

1 bunch lemon basil [*bai mangluk*], as accompaniment

¼ cup dried chili flakes, as accompaniment

1 cup vegetable stock or water

1½ cups firm silken tofu, well drained

4 cups coconut milk

3 tablespoons light soy sauce, or more to taste

½ teaspoon salt

1 cup coconut cream

Ladle the curry sauce into a serving bowl and serve along with all the accompaniments. To serve, each diner places a couple wads of noodles on a plate, tops them with a generous amount of the curry sauce, and sprinkles all the condiments over the noodles.

Curried Noodles

Serves 4

This dish is available inexpensively almost everywhere in the north of Thailand and is ideal for a vegetarian meal. It is served with an array of fresh and preserved vegetables as accompaniments. It has a perfect combination of a light curry without coconut milk over soft noodles and vegetables of your choice. When you haven't decided what to eat, this dish may appear conveniently right before your eyes, either at a sidewalk hawker's stand or from a wandering merchant.

SPICE PASTE:

5–8 large dried red chilies (California, New Mexico, or guajillo chilies)

3 tablespoons minced shallots

2 tablespoons minced lemongrass, tender midsection only

2 tablespoons minced garlic

1 tablespoon minced galangal

1 tablespoon minced fresh cilantro roots or stems

1 tablespoon minced fresh red Thai chilies (optional, for more heat)

1 teaspoon turmeric

1 teaspoon salt

Stem and seed the dried chilies. Soak them in warm water for 10–15 minutes or until soft. Drain and squeeze dry.

Using a mortar and pestle, pound and grind all the paste ingredients, starting with the chilies and adding one ingredient at a time until the mixture forms a smooth paste. Alternatively, combine all of the ingredients in a food processor and process into a smooth paste, adding a small amount of water to facilitate blending.

Bring 5 cups of water to a boil in a medium saucepan. Add the noodles and cook 5–7 minutes or until soft. Drain, rinse with cold water, and drain again. Portion the noodles into 3-ounce small wads, each about the size of a small bird's nest, and set aside.

Place the oil in a saucepan over medium heat. Add the sliced garlic and fry 3–5 minutes or until light brown and crispy. Do not burn. Remove from the oil and drain on absorbent paper or paper towels. With the same oil, fry the small dried chilies for 2–3 minutes or until crispy. Drain on absorbent paper or paper towels. Both the fried garlic and chilies are served as accompaniments.

Arrange all the accompaniments on a serving platter.

In the same oil, stir in the spice paste and cook 3–5 minutes or until fragrant. Add the tofu and mushrooms, and stir to coat well with the spice paste.

Add the vegetable stock, cherry tomatoes, light soy sauce, sweet soy sauce, and salt, and bring to a boil. Reduce the heat and simmer for 15–20 minutes. Adjust the flavor with more seasonings to taste.

Ladle the curry sauce into a serving bowl and serve along with the accompaniments.

To serve, each diner places a couple wads of noodles on a serving plate, tops them with a generous amount of the curry sauce, sprinkles all the condiments on top of the noodles, and finishes with a squeeze of fresh lime juice.

NOODLES, SAUCE, AND ACCOMPANIMENTS:

1 pound dried *kanom jeen* noodles or Japanese somen noodles

1/4 cup vegetable oil, or more as needed

2 tablespoons thinly sliced garlic, as accompaniment

6 small dried chilies, as accompaniment

2 cups fresh bean sprouts, as accompaniment

1 package (10 ounces) chopped pickled mustard greens (optional), as accompaniment

1 whole lime, cut into 6 wedges, as accompaniment

6 sprigs fresh cilantro, as accompaniment

3 stems green onions, cut into 1-inch long strips, as accompaniment

2 cups diced firm tofu, in 1/8-inch cubes

2 cups sliced mushrooms of your choice, in bite-size pieces

4 cups vegetable stock or water

2 cups chopped cherry tomatoes

2 tablespoons light soy sauce, or more to taste

2 tablespoons sweet soy sauce or fermented yellow bean sauce

1/2 teaspoon salt

Gaeng Koa Pineapple Curry

Serves 6

Pineapple, coconut, and curry are a perfect combination that will awaken your taste buds. Sweet, sour, creamy, and spicy are balanced in this refreshing yet hearty dish. Gaeng koa is one version of red curry, but it has fewer spices and less complicated flavors, which allows the ingredients, such as the pineapple in this recipe, to shine.

Combine ½ cup of the coconut milk with the curry paste in a medium saucepan. Simmer 3–5 minutes or until fragrant. Add the lemongrass, kaffir lime leaves, and the remainder of the coconut milk. Bring the mixture to a boil.

Stir in the pineapple, water chestnuts, palm sugar, light soy sauce, and vegetable base, and simmer for 10 minutes. Add the tomatoes and continue cooking 2 minutes longer or until the vegetables are tender. Adjust the flavor with more seasonings to taste.

Garnish with the basil leaves and red bell peppers before serving. Serve with steamed rice.

3 cups coconut milk

⅓ cup Gaeng Koa Curry Paste, page 43, or 3 tablespoons ready-made paste

1 stalk lemongrass, cut into 2-inch-long pieces and bruised

3 pieces kaffir lime leaves

3 cups diced pineapple, in ½-inch cubes (about 1 small pineapple)

2 cups diced water chestnuts, in ½-inch cubes (about 1 pound)

3 tablespoons palm sugar, or more to taste

3 tablespoons light soy sauce

1 tablespoon vegetable base, or 1 vegetable bouillon cube

1 cup julienne seeded tomatoes

Salt

5 sprigs fresh Thai sweet basil [*bai horapha*], leaves only, for garnish

¼ cup julienne red bell peppers, for garnish

Green Curry

Serves 6

This popular soup distinguishes itself with a pungent green curry and sweet coconut milk; as the name implies, keow is green and wan is sweet. Its curry paste is made from fresh green chilies of both mild and hot temperament, differing from most Thai curries, which are made with dried chilies. The dish is usually served with jasmine rice, but the Thai enjoy it equally when eaten with rice noodles called kanom jeen.

2 tablespoons vegetable oil

1/3 cup Green Curry Paste, page 44,
    or 3 tablespoons ready-made paste

1 1/2 cups diced Asian or Thai eggplants,
    in 1/2-inch cubes

1 1/2 cups diced zucchini, in 1/2-inch cubes

1 1/2 cups sliced long beans, in 1 1/2-inch lengths

1 1/2 cups julienne bamboo shoots
    (one 15-ounce can)

3 cups coconut milk

1/4 cup light soy sauce, or more to taste

3 tablespoons palm sugar, or more to taste

6 whole kaffir lime leaves

1 tablespoon vegetable base, or 1 vegetable
    bouillon cube

2 sprigs Thai sweet basil [*bai horapha*],
    leaves only, for garnish

1/4 cup julienne red jalapeño or red bell peppers,
    for garnish

Heat the oil in a medium saucepan over medium heat. Add the curry paste and cook 3–5 minutes or until fragrant. Add the eggplants, zucchini, long beans, and bamboo shoots and stir to mix well with the curry paste.

Add the coconut milk and bring the mixture to a boil. Stir in the soy sauce, sugar, kaffir lime leaves, and vegetable base. Reduce the heat and simmer for 7–10 minutes or until the vegetables are tender. Adjust the flavor with more seasonings to taste.

Transfer to a serving bowl and garnish with the basil and peppers.

Long Bean Wrapped Mushrooms
with Curry

Serves 4

Thaou Pun Hed

Red curry is the most versatile paste in Thai cooking. Many dishes—soups, stir-fries, and sauces—are made with red curry paste that is combined with any vegetable. On holy days, monks in Buddhist monasteries often find the meal offerings comprised of three or four kinds of red curry dishes. (See photo, facing page 161.)

2–3 large portobello mushroom caps

3–4 tablespoons vegetable oil, or more as needed

15 whole Asian long beans, both green and purple if available

1 tablespoon finely shredded fresh kaffir lime leaves (about 2 leaves)

¼ cup Red Curry Paste, page 50, or 3 tablespoons ready-made paste

¼ cup vegetable stock or water

3 tablespoons light soy sauce

2 tablespoons sugar

1 tablespoon vegetable base, or 1 vegetable bouillon cube

½ cup julienne red bell peppers, for garnish

3 sprigs Thai sweet basil [*bai horapha*], leaves only, for garnish

Cut the mushroom caps into ½ x ½ x 2-inch pieces (about 15 pieces). Heat 1–2 tablespoons of the oil in a skillet over medium heat. Add the mushrooms and fry 3–5 minutes or until light brown on all sides. Set aside on absorbent paper or paper towels.

Fill a medium saucepan with 4 cups of water. Bring to a boil, add the long beans, and simmer 2–3 minutes or until they are soft and pliable. Drain and pat dry. Trim off the tips of the stems.

Wrap a piece of mushroom widthwise with one of the long beans, making several loops around the mushroom; tuck in both ends securely. Repeat until all the mushrooms and long beans have been used. Keep them warm or heat later in a microwave.

To shred the kaffir lime leaves, stack a couple of leaves and roll them tightly into a cigarette-like roll. Slice across the roll to make fine, paper-thin strips. Set aside.

To make the sauce, heat 2 tablespoons of the oil in a medium saucepan over medium heat. Add the red curry paste and cook 2 minutes or until fragrant. Stir in the vegetable stock, light soy sauce, sugar, and vegetable base. Cook and stir for 3–5 minutes or until the sauce has reduced to a gravy.

To serve, pour the sauce over the bottom of a serving platter and arrange the warm wrapped mushrooms over the sauce. Sprinkle with the shredded kaffir lime leaves and garnish with the red bell peppers and basil leaves.

Massamun Curry

Gaeng Massamun

Dating back to the ancient kingdom of Ayudthaya, King Narai, who was fond of Indian food, imported a chef for his royal kitchen. From the royal court, the aromatic massamun curry made it into the mainstream Thai diet, and its paste still contains an extraordinary variety of Indian herbs and spices.

1 cup coconut cream

1/3 cup Massamun Curry Paste, page 46, or 1/4 cup ready-made paste

1 pound small new potatoes, peeled

1 pound pearl onions, peeled

1 pound peeled and diced carrots, in 1/4-inch cubes

3 cups coconut milk

1 1/2 cups diced pineapple, in 1/2-inch cubes (optional)

1/2 cup whole roasted peanuts

1/2 cup tamarind liquid

1/4 cup light soy sauce, or more to taste

3 tablespoons palm sugar, or more to taste

1 tablespoon vegetable base, or 1 vegetable bouillon cube

3 whole cardamom seeds

3 whole bay leaves

1 cinnamon stick

Heat 1/2 cup of the coconut cream in a medium saucepan over medium heat (reserve the remaining 1/2 cup of coconut cream for a topping). Stir in the curry paste and cook 3–5 minutes or until fragrant. Stir in the rest of the ingredients, except for the reserved coconut cream, and bring to a boil.

Reduce the heat and simmer 10–15 minutes or until the vegetables are tender. Remove from the heat and top with the reserved 1/2 cup of coconut cream. Serve with steamed rice.

Red Curry

Serves 6

This dish is the most often cooked curry in the Thai household. If a home chef can't decide which curry to prepare that would please all family members, he or she will end up making red curry. Its paste can be easily made from staple ingredients in the Thai pantry, such as dried chilies, garlic, shallots, and dried herbs and spices. The paste also pairs well with nearly all ingredients, especially any vegetables that grow near the house or those that have been left in the refrigerator.

2 tablespoons vegetable oil

$1/3$ cup Red Curry Paste, page 50, or 3 tablespoons ready-made paste

$1 1/2$ cups diced Asian or Thai eggplants, in $1/2$-inch cubes

$1 1/2$ cups sliced tofu sheets or skins, in bite-size pieces

$1 1/2$ cups sliced long beans, in $1 1/2$-inch lengths

$1 1/2$ cups julienne bamboo shoots (one 15-ounce can)

3 cups coconut milk

$1/4$ cup light soy sauce, or more to taste

3 tablespoons palm sugar, or more to taste

6 whole kaffir lime leaves

1 tablespoon vegetable base, or 1 vegetable bouillon cube

$1/4$ cup julienne red jalapeño or red bell peppers, for garnish

2 sprigs Thai sweet basil [*bai horapha*], leaves only, for garnish

Heat the oil in a medium saucepan over medium heat. Add the curry paste and cook 3–5 minutes or until fragrant. Add the eggplants, tofu sheets, long beans, and bamboo shoots and stir to mix well with the curry paste.

Add the coconut milk and bring to a boil. Stir in the soy sauce, sugar, kaffir lime leaves, and vegetable base. Reduce the heat and simmer for 7–10 minutes or until the vegetables are tender. Adjust the flavor with more seasonings to taste.

Transfer to a serving bowl and garnish with the peppers and basil leaves. Serve with steamed rice.

Morning Glory with Peanut Sauce

Serves 6

Ramayana is a popular epic; it originated in India and spread throughout Asia along with Hinduism and Buddhism. This elaborate dish carries a name of the leading male character in the story, Pra Ram. He has an emerald green complexion and is represented by morning glory, a green vegetable in this dish. Pra Ram performs an ablution, Loung Soung, and emerges fresh and clean with an anointment, symbolized by the morning glory being poached and topped with a golden curry peanut sauce.

MORNING GLORY:

2 pounds morning glory or spinach

1 pound firm tofu, drained well

3 tablespoons vegetable oil, or more as needed

PEANUT SAUCE:

2 1/2 cups coconut milk, or more as needed

1/4 cup Red Curry Paste, page 50, or 3 tablespoons ready-made paste

3 tablespoons tamarind liquid

3 tablespoons palm sugar, or more to taste

3 tablespoons light soy sauce, or more to taste

1/2 – 3/4 cup peanut paste or chunky peanut butter, or more to taste

3 tablespoons chopped roasted peanuts, for garnish

Wash the morning glory or spinach and trim off any tough stems and roots. Cut into 2-inch-long pieces. Fill a large pot halfway with water. Bring to a boil and poach the morning glory for 2 minutes. Remove from the hot water and immediately plunge into cold water. Drain well until completely dry and arrange on a serving platter.

Slice the tofu into thin, 2-inch-long pieces. Heat the oil in a skillet over medium heat. Add the tofu and cook, turning once, for 3–5 minutes or until light brown on both sides. Remove and arrange on top of the morning glory.

To make the sauce, place ½ cup of the coconut milk in a medium saucepan over medium heat. Stir in the curry paste and cook 3–5 minutes or until fragrant.

Add the remaining 2 cups of coconut milk, tamarind liquid, sugar, and soy sauce. Bring the mixture to a boil and stir in the peanut paste. Cook, stirring constantly, for 5–7 minutes or until the peanut paste has dissolved and is well combined. Be careful the mixture doesn't burn on the bottom. Adjust the flavor with more seasonings to taste. Add more coconut milk if the sauce is too thick.

To serve, reheat the morning glory and tofu in a microwave, if necessary. Top with a generous amount of peanut sauce and garnish with the chopped peanuts.

Panaeng Curry

Serves 6

Malaysia has had a strong influence on Thai cuisine, such as this dish, which originally came from the city of Penang on the southern border of Thailand. Beef is usually the choice of meat for religious reasons, as Malaysia and southern Thailand are predominantly Muslim. In the Central region, the dish has been adapted locally using all kinds of ingredients, including tofu. Whatever ingredient is used, it should be cooked until tender and the sauce fully absorbed. Shredded kaffir lime, both in the curry paste and garnish, is needed to tie all the flavors together.

2 tablespoons vegetable oil

1/3 cup Panaeng Curry Paste, page 47, or 3 tablespoons ready-made paste

2 cups diced fried or firm tofu, in 1/4-inch cubes

2 cups coconut milk

1/4 cup light soy sauce

3 tablespoons palm sugar, or more to taste

4 whole kaffir lime leaves, for garnish

I cup julienne onions

I cup julienne red bell peppers

3 tablespoons finely chopped roasted peanuts

I cup coconut cream

2 sprigs Thai sweet basil [bai horapha], leaves only, for garnish

Heat the oil in a saucepan over medium heat. Add the curry paste and cook 2–3 minutes or until fragrant. Add the tofu and stir until well coated with the curry paste.

Stir in the coconut milk, soy sauce, and palm sugar. Bring the mixture to a boil, reduce the heat, and simmer 15–20 minutes or until somewhat thickened.

Stack 4 kaffir lime leaves and roll tightly into a cigarette-like roll. Slice across the roll to make fine, paper-thin strips. Set aside for garnish.

Stir the onions, bell peppers, and roasted peanuts into the tofu mixture. Cook until the vegetables are tender, about 5 minutes longer. Stir in the coconut cream and remove from the heat. Transfer to a serving platter and garnish with the shredded kaffir lime leaves and basil leaves. Serve with steamed rice.

Yellow Curry

Serves 6

This mild curry has obvious Indian origins, not only from the coriander and cumin, but also the yellow curry powder. It is very rich and creamy, as both coconut milk and cream are used. It often requires Cucumber Salad Ajad, page 67, as an accompaniment to help clear the palate after a few bites.

3 tablespoons vegetable oil

1/4 cup thinly sliced shallots, for garnish

1/3 cup Yellow Curry Paste, page 52, or 3 tablespoons ready-made paste

2 cups coconut milk

I cup diced peeled potatoes, in 1/4-inch cubes

I cup diced peeled taro, in 1/4-inch cubes

I cup diced peeled kabocha squash or pumpkin, in 1/4-inch cubes

I cup julienne red bell peppers

1/2 cup julienne onions

1/4 cup light soy sauce, or more to taste

2 tablespoons curry powder

2 tablespoons sugar, or more to taste

I cup coconut cream

1/2 cup Thai sweet basil [*bai horapha*], leaves only, for garnish

Heat the oil in a medium saucepan over medium heat. Add the shallots and fry 2–3 minutes or until light brown and crispy. Remove and drain on absorbent paper or paper towels. Set aside for garnish.

With the same oil, add the curry paste and cook 3–5 minutes or until fragrant. Add the coconut milk, potatoes, taro, and squash and bring to a boil. Reduce the heat to low and simmer 7–10 minutes or until the vegetables are almost tender. Add the red peppers, onions, light soy sauce, curry powder, and sugar, and simmer for a few minutes longer until the vegetables are tender. Adjust the flavor with more soy sauce and sugar to taste. Remove from the heat and stir in the coconut cream.

Transfer to a serving bowl and garnish with the fried shallots and basil leaves just before serving.

Curries and Main Dishes

Red Curry Fried Cakes

Serves 6

Versatile red curry paste is used in this dish, adding deep flavor to rather plain silken tofu. The moisture content in this recipe, especially in the tofu, is crucial, as it can make or break the texture of the cakes. Too much water, the texture will be too soft and unable to form a cake; not enough water, it will fall apart. For this reason, make sure to extract as much water as possible from the tofu.

RED CURRY FRIED CAKES:

4 whole kaffir lime leaves

1 pound firm silken tofu, well drained

1/4 cup Red Curry Paste, page 50, or 3 tablespoons ready-made paste

3 tablespoons sugar

2 tablespoons cornstarch

1 tablespoon vegetable base, or 1 vegetable bouillon cube, finely crumbled

1 tablespoon light soy sauce, or more to taste

1/2 teaspoon salt

3/4 cup thinly sliced long beans, in round slivers

3 cups vegetable oil for deep-frying

To finely shred the kaffir lime leaves, stack the 4 leaves and roll them tightly into a cigarette-like roll. Slice across the roll to make fine, paper-thin strips.

Transfer to a food processor and add all the remaining cake ingredients except the long beans and oil. Process into a thick paste. Transfer to a bowl and fold in the long beans. Cover and refrigerate for at least 30 minutes.

Place the oil in a deep pan and heat to 375°F. The oil should have a depth of at least two inches. With damp hands, form the mixture into thin patties about one inch in diameter and one-quarter-inch thick. Gently drop the patties into the pan to fit loosely. Deep-fry the patties, turning once, for 4–6 minutes or until golden brown on all sides. Remove and drain on absorbent paper or paper towels. Serve the fried cakes with Dipping Sauce (recipe follows).

To make the dipping sauce, combine the water, sugar, and soy sauce in a medium saucepan over medium heat. Simmer for 5–7 minutes or until the mixture is reduced to a thin syrup. Remove from the heat and let cool.

Ten minutes before serving, add the remainder of the ingredients, except the cilantro, and stir to combine well. Add more salt to taste, if desired. Serve as a sauce for the fried cakes. Garnish with the fresh cilantro leaves.

DIPPING SAUCE:

$1/4$ cup water

$1/3$ cup sugar

2 tablespoons light soy sauce

2 cups thinly sliced English cucumbers, in half circles

I cup julienne red bell peppers

$1/4$ cup rice vinegar or fresh lime juice

$1/4$ cup chopped roasted peanuts

$1/4$ teaspoon salt

2 teaspoons minced garlic

I teaspoon minced fresh Thai chilies, more or less to taste

5 sprigs fresh cilantro, leaves only, for garnish

Steamed Curry in Banana Bowls

Serves 6

Curry mousse is rather a familiar description for this dish. Rich coconut cream is beaten and incorporated with red curry paste, and silken tofu and cornstarch are added as binding agents instead of eggs. Steaming provides extra moisture and helps achieve the silky smooth, custard-like texture.

1 package frozen banana leaves (5–6 ounces)

4 kaffir lime leaves

2 cups shredded napa cabbage

1 1/2 cups firm silken tofu, well drained and crumbled

1/4 cup Red Curry Paste, page 50, or 3 tablespoons ready-made paste

2 tablespoons sugar

2 tablespoons light soy sauce

1 tablespoon vegetable base, or 1 vegetable bouillon cube, finely crumbled

2 cups coconut cream

2 cups inoki mushrooms, roots trimmed

3 tablespoons cornstarch

1/4 teaspoon salt

6 sprigs fresh cilantro, leaves only, for garnish

1/4 cup julienne red jalapeño or bell peppers

To make banana bowls (6 pieces), cut the banana leaves into 12 round pieces with a 7–8-inch diameter. For each bowl, stack 2 pieces to double the thickness and fold up the edges to form a bowl. Help the bowls hold their shape by using toothpicks or staples. If you prefer, small ramekins can be used instead of the banana bowls.

To finely shred the kaffir lime leaves, stack the 4 leaves and roll them tightly into a cigarette-like roll. Slice across the roll to make fine, paper-thin strips.

Place 3 cups of water in a medium saucepan over medium heat and bring to a boil. Add the shredded napa cabbage and poach for 2 minutes. Drain and rinse with cold water. Squeeze out as much water as possible from the napa cabbage and distribute it evenly to line the bottom of the banana bowls.

Combine the tofu, curry paste, sugar, soy sauce, and vegetable base in a medium bowl. Stir in 1½ cups of the coconut cream in ½-cup increments, stirring vigorously and constantly until well mixed. Add the mushrooms, 2 tablespoons of the cornstarch, and the shredded kaffir lime leaves. Stir to mix well. Fill the banana bowls with this mixture and arrange on a steamer rack.

Combine the remaining ½ cup of coconut cream, the remaining 1 tablespoon of cornstarch, and the salt in a small bowl. Spread about a tablespoon of this mixture over each curry bowl and garnish with the cilantro leaves and jalapeño peppers.

Steam the curry bowls over boiling water in a steamer with a tight-fitting lid (or in a bamboo steamer set) for 10–15 minutes or until firm and hot. Serve with steamed jasmine rice.

Yellow Spiced Rice

Serves 6

Traveling through Southeast Asia, I've seen this dish in Indonesia, Malaysia, Myanmar, Singapore, and Thailand. Each version has subtle differences according to the local tastes, but the main influence must have been from Persia and India, as a similar dish shows up in those cuisines.

3 tablespoons vegetable oil

2 tablespoons minced shallots

2 cups long-grain aromatic rice (Thai jasmine or Indian basmati rice)

2 cups vegetable stock, or 1 tablespoon vegetable base mixed with 2 cups of water

1 1/2 cups coconut milk

2 tablespoons turmeric

2 tablespoons sugar

1 teaspoon ground coriander

1 teaspoon ground cumin

1 cinnamon stick

2 whole kaffir lime leaves or bay leaves

3 whole cloves

1 teaspoon salt

If using a rice cooker, combine all the ingredients and stir to mix well. Press the "on" switch and let cook undisturbed for 45 minutes. Fluff the rice and discard the cinnamon stick, kaffir lime leaves, and cloves before serving.

If using a saucepan, heat the oil and add the shallots. Cook until fragrant, about 2 minutes. Add the rice and stir until the grains are well coated with oil. Add the rest of ingredients and bring to a boil. Reduce the heat to medium-low and cover with a lid. Cook the rice undisturbed for 10–15 minutes or until fully cooked and all the liquid is absorbed. Turn off the heat and let stand on the still hot range for 10 minutes. Fluff the rice and discard the cinnamon stick, kaffir lime leaves, and cloves before serving.

Desserts, Sweets, and Beverages

In Thailand, most desserts are also served as snacks or light meals that can be eaten anytime. Fried bananas and sweet rice with mango, for example, are served at all hours and are not necessarily eaten at the end of the meal.

Thai savory dishes are highlighted internationally, but unfortunately, Thai desserts fall below par. Most Thai desserts hardly suit the Western palate because of their rich coconut, plain sweetness, and generally heavy texture. But Thai fruits make up for the lack of popularity of the desserts in their quality, variety, and exciting flavors.

During the ancient time of Siam, sweets and desserts were not daily items for the majority of agricultural households. Sweet offerings were for special occasions, such as weddings and funerals, and they were often part of a donation to Buddhist monks on weekends and holy days. Only well-to-do families had the luxury of sweet treats and, most importantly, the royal kitchen was the center for the development of Thai desserts, but then only for a small group of royalty and bureaucrats.

In the new dawn of Thailand, when trade with foreign countries brought an influx of cultural exchanges and the growing royal government employed more ordinary people, Thai desserts had a greater dietary impact on the majority of Thai people. By mixing and matching ingredients and techniques, both local and foreign, Thai sweets became prevalent as snacks, light meals, and after dinner desserts. Recipes were modified, diversified, and categorized as never before; cake and ice cream stimulated and accessorized the Thai palate and language.

Coconut is the spirit that gives Thai desserts their creamy, buttery flavor. The cattle industry has only recently become established in Thailand, producing milk, cream, and butter. Before then, only coconut products were used. Coconut imparts a rich, creamy, buttery taste to Thai desserts; it also adds a unique sweet flavor. Coconut or palm sugar comes from the sweet sap of coconut inflorescences and is indispensable in Thai desserts.

The final ingredient that makes Thai desserts authentic is Thai fragrance. Jasmine shrub and pandan bush (screw pine) are native to Thailand and their jasmine water and pandan liquid add a sweet aroma that distinguishes Thai cakes and desserts.

Somehow, among the many kinds of desserts offered in Thai cuisine, no more than a handful make it to the United States and international markets. These dishes, the pioneers of Thai desserts, are being adapted to suit the Western palate. Hopefully, in the not too distant future, all Thai desserts will gain their much-deserved spotlight.

Banana Pudding in Coconut Cream

Serves 6

Thai banana trees produce fruit year-round. In addition to eating the bananas ripe and fresh, Thais cook them with coconut cream and sugar to make a banana pudding. This is an easy and quick recipe for a satisfying sweet and creamy dessert. The Thai name kluai buat chee *means "bananas turned nuns," as the white color of this dessert symbolizes Buddhist nuns that are wearing only white clothes.*

10–15 whole Thai bananas [*kluai nam wa*] or baby bananas [*kluai khai*], or 5–7 large regular bananas

3 cups coconut milk

3/4 cup sugar, or more to taste

1 teaspoon salt, or more to taste

1 teaspoon pandan extract or vanilla extract

1/2 cup coconut cream

Select bananas that are not fully ripe. Peel the bananas and cut in half lengthwise. Slice into 1 x 2-inch pieces. You should have 3–4 cups of pieces.

Place the coconut milk in a medium saucepan over medium heat and bring to a boil. Add the bananas and cook 4–5 minutes.

Add the sugar, salt, and pandan extract. Stir gently until the sugar is dissolved and cook for 3–5 minutes longer. Remove from the heat and stir in the coconut cream. Serve the pudding warm.

Banana Purée Cake

Serves 6

Bananas are easy to obtain and their trees produce fruit in abundance. A surplus of overripe bananas is utilized to make this simple cake, which is equivalent to banana bread in the United States.

2 overripe large regular bananas
3 overripe Thai bananas [*kluai nam wa*]
5 overripe baby bananas [*kluai kai*]
1/2 cup rice flour
1/2 cup cornstarch
1 cup shredded coconut
1/2 teaspoon salt
2 cups coconut cream
1 cup sugar
1 pint coconut or vanilla ice cream (optional)

Purée the bananas in a food processor to make 3–4 cups. Add the rice flour and cornstarch and process into a smooth paste. Set aside.

Combine the shredded coconut and salt in a small bowl. In a separate large bowl, combine the coconut cream and sugar. Stir until the sugar is dissolved. Stir in the banana purée and half of the salted shredded coconut. Mix well.

Transfer the mixture to an 8 x 8 x 2-inch square pan. Alternatively, small ramekins may be used. Spread the mixture evenly and sprinkle with the remaining salted shredded coconut. Steam in a steamer rack over boiling water for 20–25 minutes or until firm. A large wok with a lid and an inserted rack can also be used as a steamer.

Remove from the heat and let cool. Cut the banana purée cake into bite-size pieces or serve whole in the ramekins. Serve the cake warm or at room temperature with ice cream à la mode, if desired.

Black Beans in Coconut Cream

Serves 6

Thao Dam Gaeng Buat

Dried peanuts are as popular in Thai savory dishes as dried mung beans are in Thai desserts. The use of other dried beans in recipes, however, is few and far between. Thais prefer to cook with fresh, young, tender beans or peas rather than their dried seeds. This dish is one of the very few exceptions where alternative beans are used in a Thai dessert. In the United States, any dried beans can be used; soaking and cooking times will vary depending on the size, age, and texture of the bean.

1 cup dried black beans
3 cups coconut milk
2/3 cup palm sugar, or more to taste
1/2 cup coconut cream
1/2 teaspoon salt

Soak the beans in plenty of cold water to cover for least 3 hours or overnight. Drain.

Combine the beans with 6 cups of fresh water in a medium saucepan and bring to a boil. Reduce the heat, cover, and simmer for 20 minutes or until the beans are so tender that they can be mashed between your fingers. Drain and set aside.

Combine the coconut milk and palm sugar in the same saucepan and bring to a gentle boil to make coconut syrup. Stir in the cooked beans and continue cooking 10–15 minutes or until the beans have fully absorbed the coconut syrup.

Combine the coconut cream and salt in a small bowl and stir to mix well.

To serve, ladle the beans into individual serving bowls and sprinkle with the salted coconut cream. Serve warm or at room temperature.

Coconut Ice Cream

Serves 6

Cold desserts came very late in Thai cuisine, especially ice cream, which was unknown until the arrival of trade with Europeans and technology. Homemade, freshly squeezed coconut milk makes a refreshing difference.

I-teem Kati

1–2 ripe coconuts, or 3 ½ cups fresh coconut milk
1 cup sugar
⅓ cup water

For the best results, freshly squeezed coconut milk is preferable for a refreshing, sweet flavor. Crack the ripe coconuts and shred the white meat into fine flakes or extract the white meat from the shell and process it in a food processor until it forms a paste.

Combine the processed coconut meat with 1 cup of hot water in a large bowl. Steep the coconut for 5–6 minutes and then knead and squeeze coconut milk from the mixture. Strain the mixture through a fine sieve to get the rich coconut milk. Repeat the process with more hot water until you obtain about 3½ cups of coconut milk.

Combine the sugar with the water in a small saucepan and simmer over medium heat until reduced to a thick syrup (it should coat the back of a spoon). Remove from the heat and let cool to lukewarm. Add the coconut milk and stir to mix well.

Pour into an ice cream maker and process until stiff, about 45 minutes. Coconut ice cream must be kept very cold because it melts rapidly.

For extra flavor and texture, add sliced fruits (such as jackfruit, lychee, and/or young coconut) to the mixture before freezing.

Crunchy "Ruby" Water Chestnuts

Serves 6

Tubtim Krop

Precious stones of prosperity is the underlying concept for this dessert. A variety of fruit whose color represents a precious stone is used in this dish; for example, yellow jackfruit symbolizes gold, clear longan symbolizes diamonds, and water chestnuts dyed red symbolize rubies. Good fortune is bestowed upon those who eat this sweet and creamy dessert.

1 1/2 cups fresh water chestnuts (1 pound)

2 tablespoons red food coloring

1/2 cup cornstarch, or more as needed

1 cup sugar

2 tablespoons water

2 cups coconut cream

1 teaspoon jasmine, pandan, rose, or vanilla extract

2 cups diced assorted tropical fruits, in 1/4-inch cubes (jackfruit, longan, lychee, etc.)

2 cups crushed ice

Peel the water chestnuts and dice them into 1/8-inch cubes. Rinse with cold water. Transfer to a large bowl and sprinkle with the food coloring to create light and dark red spots that imitate the look of rubies or pomegranate seeds. Add 2 cups of cold water and soak the water chestnuts for at least 2 hours.

Drain and pat completely dry with towels. Fold in the cornstarch to coat evenly. Transfer to a sieve or colander and shake off the excess starch.

Bring 4 cups of water to a gentle boil in a medium saucepan. Scatter in a small batch of the coated water chestnuts. Gently stir once so they do not stick to each other and cook until they float to the surface. Remove the water chestnuts with a slotted spoon or wire strainer and immediately plunge them into a bowl of cold water. Continue with the next small batch of water chestnuts. When they are all completely cold, transfer them to a colander to drain the water.

To make the syrup, combine the sugar with the water in a small saucepan. Simmer until the sugar is dissolved and the mixture turns into a thick syrup (about the consistency of maple syrup). Remove from the heat and let cool. Stir in the coconut cream and the extract and mix well.

To serve, combine the water chestnuts, assorted fruits, and coconut syrup. Portion the mixture into serving bowls and top with the crushed ice.

Floating Lotus

Serves 6

Bua Loi Sawan

White and pink lotus flowers dot rural areas of the Thai landscape. Wherever there is water, there are lotus flowers, either in ponds, reservoirs, or planting fields. The fresh, young, and crunchy seeds of the lotus can be eaten as a snack. Dried seeds can be ground into lotus flour. They also can be boiled whole and served with syrup, or boiled and processed into a paste, as in this recipe. Lotus seeds have a unique flavor and sweet fragrance that goes well in desserts.

LOTUS BALLS:

½ cup dried lotus seeds, shelled and split

1 ½ cups sweet rice flour, or more as needed

½ cup boiling hot water, or more as needed

1 teaspoon pandan, jasmine, rose, or vanilla extract

COCONUT SYRUP:

2 cups coconut milk

⅔ cup palm sugar, or more to taste

½ teaspoon salt

½ cup coconut cream

1 teaspoon pandan, jasmine, rose, or vanilla extract

Soak the lotus seeds in plenty of cold water for at least 2 hours. Drain and transfer to a small saucepan. Add 3 cups of water and bring to a boil. Simmer 20–25 minutes or until the seeds are tender. Drain. Transfer to a food processor and process into a smooth paste.

Combine the lotus paste, sweet rice flour, hot water, and pandan extract in a large bowl. Mix with a spoon until cool enough to handle with your hands. Dust your hands with extra rice flour and knead the dough until it is smooth and easy to handle. Add more flour or water if needed. Roll the dough into small balls, each ¼ inch in diameter.

Place 5 cups of water in a medium saucepan and bring to a boil. Sprinkle the lotus balls into the boiling water, a small batch at a time, and cook 2–3 minutes until they float to the surface. Remove from the hot water using a wire strainer or slotted spoon and plunge into a bowl of cold water to prevent them from sticking to each other. Drain in a colander.

Combine the coconut milk, palm sugar, and salt in a medium saucepan. Simmer, stirring often, until the sugar is dissolved. Bring to a boil and add the cooked lotus balls. Return to a boil. Remove from the heat and stir in the coconut cream and extract. Serve warm or at room temperature. *Vegetable Satay, page 81*

Fried Bananas

Serves 6

Klaui Tod

Whether as a snack, a meal, or a dessert, fried bananas can serve all purposes. Walking along the streets of Thailand, you can't miss this popular offering, smoldering hot from the deep-fry pan of hawker stores. In addition to bananas, sweet potatoes and taro can also be used, adding more varieties of taste and texture.

BATTER:

1 cup all-purpose flour, or more as needed

1/2 cup rice flour

1/2 cup sweetened coconut flakes or shredded coconut

1/2 cup coconut milk

1/2 cup water, or more as needed

1/3 cup sugar, more or less to taste

2 tablespoons sesame seeds

2 teaspoons baking powder

2 teaspoons salt

BANANAS AND CONDIMENTS:

15 Thai bananas [*kluai nam wa*], or 7–8 large regular bananas or plantains

4 cups vegetable oil, for frying

1/4 cup honey

2 tablespoons powdered sugar

1 whole lime, cut into 6 wedges

1 pint coconut or vanilla ice cream (optional)

Combine all the batter ingredients in a bowl and stir to mix well. Add more flour or water as needed to make a smooth, thick, pancake-like batter.

Choose bananas that are not fully ripe. Peel and cut into pieces 1/4-inch thick by 2 inches long. Place the oil in a deep frying pan or wok and heat to 350°F. The oil should have a depth of at least two inches.

Dip the bananas in the batter, turning to coat evenly. Carefully lower the bananas into the hot oil, adding just enough to fit loosely. Fry the bananas 5–7 minutes, turning once, until they are golden brown and crispy on each side. Remove the bananas with a slotted spoon or wire strainer and drain on absorbent paper or paper towels.

To serve, drizzle the fried bananas with the honey and dust with the powdered sugar. Serve with lime wedges and ice cream à la mode, if desired. Diners can squeeze the lime over their individual servings.

Long Bean Wrapped Mushrooms, pages 140-141

Layer Cakes

Serves 6

Layer cakes and climbing a career ladder are synonymous in Thai culture, as building up a cake layer is the same as advancing a step in a career path. This cake is often served during a celebration of getting a promotion or a raise. The cake with nine layers is the ultimate achievement as it represents the pinnacle of the career.

3 cups sugar

1 cup warm water

1 cup rice flour

1 cup tapioca flour

2 ½ cups coconut cream

2 teaspoons condensed pandan extract with an intense green color

¼ teaspoon green food coloring (optional)

¼ cup vegetable oil, for brushing

Combine the sugar and water in a small saucepan and place over medium heat. Simmer until the mixture turns into a thin syrup (thinner than maple syrup). Let cool to lukewarm.

Combine the rice flour and tapioca flour in a medium bowl. Stir in the syrup and mix well. Slowly add the coconut cream, a little at a time, and stir until well combined.

Divide the mixture into two equal portions. Add the pandan extract to one portion and stir to get an even color (add the green food coloring if the pandan extract is not green enough to get a light green mixture). Leave the other portion white.

Place an 8 x 8 x 2-inch pan in a steamer and brush the pan lightly with oil. Pour a small amount of the white mixture into the pan, spreading it evenly into a thin layer, about ⅛-inch thick. Make sure that the pan sits very level in the steamer. Cover the steamer with a lid and steam this first layer of the cake for 7–8 minutes or until firm.

Open the lid and lightly brush the firm first layer with oil to make it shiny. Pour a small batch of the green mixture over the white first layer, spreading evenly into another thin (⅛-inch thick) layer. Cover with the lid and steam 7–8 minutes or until firm.

Continue the process to make 8 or 9 layers of cake, alternating the colors, finishing with the last green layer on the top. Let cool. Cut the layer cake into squares or diamond-shaped pieces. Serve cold or at room temperature.

Longan Drink

Serves 6

Nam Lumyai

One of Thailand's most popular early summer fresh fruits is longans [lumyai], whose sweet and aromatic flavor is always highly anticipated. Fresh longan fruit is round, the size of a cherry, with leathery brown skin. It has an opaque white meat and a round black marble-like seed. Dried longan is available all year round and is popular for an ice-cold drink.

4 ounces dried, seedless longan [*lumyai*]

1 cup sugar

4 cups crushed ice

Place 4 cups of water in a medium saucepan and bring to a boil over medium heat. Add the dried longan and cook for 10–15 minutes or until the longan is fully expanded. Stir in the sugar and remove from the heat. Let cool.

To serve, fill glasses with crushed ice and top with the longan syrup.

Mung Bean Wraps

Serves 6 (makes 20 pieces)

Thoa Paay

Small yellow mung beans are used often in Thai desserts. This elaborate recipe has many simple steps: preparing the dough and filling, wrapping, cooking, and assembling to serve. This dish is a good example of most Thai desserts that are time consuming to make with tiny, intricate details, but they usually employ simple cooking techniques.

DOUGH:

1 1/2 cups sweet rice flour

1/2 cup rice flour, or more as needed

3/4 cup boiling hot water, or more as needed

1 teaspoon pandan, jasmine, rose, or vanilla extract

MUNG BEAN STUFFING:

1/2 cup dried split yellow mung beans

1/2 cup shredded coconut

1/2 cup sugar

1/3 teaspoon salt

Combine the flours in a large bowl and mix well. Slowly pour the hot water over the flour and gently mix with a large spoon. Stir in the extract and mix well to make a dough. When the dough is cool enough to handle with your bare hands, knead until soft and smooth, adding more flour or water as needed. Roll and form the dough into 20 small balls, each about 1 inch in diameter. Press each ball into a flat, round disk, about 2 inches in diameter.

Bring 10 cups of water to a boil in a large pot. Add 4–5 dough disks to the pot and cook until they float to the surface. Remove the disks from the pot with a wire strainer or slotted spoon and transfer them to a tray. Immediately fill the center of the disks with about 1 tablespoon of the Mung Bean Stuffing (recipe follows) and fold into a half circle. While the dough is still hot and gluey, roll it in a tray or plate of Shredded Coconut Topping (recipe follows). The coconut should completely coat the dough and prevent the pieces from sticking to each other. Arrange the pieces on a serving platter, and just before serving sprinkle with the Sesame Seed Topping (recipe follows).

Alternatively, instead of boiling the disks first, fill each with 1 tablespoon of the Mung Bean Stuffing, fold into a half circle, and press the edges together, making sure the dough is sealed tightly. Cook the wrapped dough in boiling water until they float to the surface. While the dough is still hot, roll it in the Shredded Coconut Topping. Arrange the pieces on a serving platter, and just before serving sprinkle with the Sesame Seed Topping.

SHREDDED COCONUT TOPPING:
1 1/2 cups shredded coconut
1/8 teaspoon salt

SESAME SEED TOPPING:
3/4 cup sugar
1/2 cup roasted black and white sesame seeds

To make the Mung Bean Stuffing, soak the beans in cold water to cover for at least 3 hours or overnight. Drain. Transfer to a large pot and add 3 cups of fresh water. Bring to a boil and simmer until tender enough that they can be mashed between your fingers. Do not overcook to the point that they are soft and disintegrated. Drain well. Combine the cooked beans, shredded coconut, sugar, and salt in a large bowl.

To make the Shredded Coconut Topping, combine the coconut and salt in a small bowl. Spread out evenly on a tray so the warm cooked mung bean wraps can be easily rolled in it.

To make the Sesame Seed Topping, combine the sugar and sesame seeds in a small bowl.

Pandan Sweet Jelly

Serves 6 (makes 12 pieces)

Every cuisine has its own jelly dish, and Thais have this one as their most popular jelly dessert. Agar-agar is the Malay name of a seaweed by-product, which is a powerful gel-former (it will set even at room temperature), owing to the unusual length of its carbohydrate molecules. Thais use agar-agar powder [woon pong] in their desserts and especially enjoy adding all kinds of seasonal fruits to this see-through dish.

BOTTOM LAYER:

1 bunch fresh pandan leaves, or 2½ teaspoons pandan extract

1 tablespoon agar-agar powder [*woon pong*]

1 cup sugar

1 cup diced tropical fruits of your choice: jackfruit, longan, or lychee (optional)

12 small molds, each 3 inches in diameter and at least 2 inches deep (any shape, although flowers or animals are usually used)

Slice the pandan leaves into small strips and then bruise or pound them with the back of a knife. Bring 4 cups of water to a boil in a medium saucepan. Add the bruised pandan leaves and simmer for 8–10 minutes or until the water turns green with intense fragrance. Strain and discard the solids. Measure out 2½ cups of the pandan water and reserve the remainder. If using the pandan extract, dilute it in 2½ cups of water.

Combine the agar-agar powder and the 2½ cups of pandan water in a medium saucepan and bring to a boil. Add the sugar and stir to dissolve. If using the diced fruits, wait until the agar-agar mixture is lukewarm before adding them. Pour the mixture into the molds to fill them three-quarters full and then refrigerate 10–15 minutes or until set and firm.

To make the top layer, combine the pandan water and agar-agar in a medium pot. Place over medium heat and bring to a boil. Add the sugar and stir to dissolve.

Stir in the coconut cream and salt and mix well. Reduce the heat to low and simmer, stirring occasionally, for 2–3 minutes.

Pour the mixture over the cold bottom layer in the molds and chill in the refrigerator until set and firm, about 20 minutes. Unmold. The finished jelly should be light green on top and white on the bottom. You can reverse the colors by reversing the process. Decorate with the optional orchid flowers or rose petals, if desired.

TOP LAYER:

1 cup pandan water, or 1 teaspoon pandan extract mixed with 1 cup water

1 tablespoon plain, unflavored agar-agar powder [*woon pong*]

1/2 cup sugar

1 1/2 cups coconut cream

1/3 teaspoon salt

12 orchid flowers or rose petals, for decoration

Sticky Rice and Mangoes

Serves 6

This is the most popular dessert in Thai cuisine. Thais would happily eat it anytime, in addition to enjoying it at the end of a meal. Sticky rice and mango can be served as a snack, a light meal, or a dessert. In Thailand, there are more than fifty different kinds of mangoes and more than a dozen kinds that are well suited for sticky rice. In the United States, only a few kinds of mangoes are available at particular times of the year. When dealing with mangoes, you have to be very selective. Sweet, ripe mangoes are essential to this dessert. A Thai cylindrical bamboo steamer is used to cook this particular rice, but a regular steamer can be used by lining it with cheesecloth.

2 cups sweet sticky long-grain rice [*khao neaw*]

1 cup palm sugar or granulated sugar

2 1/2 cups coconut cream

1 teaspoon pandan or vanilla extract

3/4 teaspoon salt

3 ripe mangoes

2 tablespoons roasted black and tan sesame seeds or roasted yellow mung beans, for garnish

Soak the rice in cold water to cover for at least 2 hours or overnight. Drain the rice and place in a steamer rack over cheesecloth, if necessary. Steam the rice over high heat for 15 minutes and turn the mass of rice over (top to bottom). Continue steaming for another 10 minutes until tender.

While the rice is steaming, place the palm sugar in a small saucepan over medium heat and cook until it is melted. Remove from the heat and stir in the coconut cream, pandan extract, and salt. Stir until the sugar is dissolved. If using granulated sugar, combine the sugar, coconut cream, pandan extract, and salt and stir until the sugar is dissolved. Set aside to later mix with the rice.

When the rice is ready, transfer it to a bowl and level the top with a wet wooden spoon. Do not pack the rice.

While the rice is still hot, pour 3/4 of the coconut mixture over the top of the rice, cover with a lid or plastic wrap, and set aside to rest for 10 minutes. Remove the lid and fold the rice with the wet wooden spoon from top to bottom to get an even texture throughout. Cover again and set aside.

To serve, peel the mangoes and slice into bite-size pieces. Arrange the rice and mango on a serving platter and top with the remaining coconut mixture. Sprinkle with the roasted sesame seeds or yellow beans before serving.

Mung Bean Drink

Serves 6

Nam Thaou Leung

If coffee is not your cup of tea, this mung bean drink could be your choice for a caffeine-free beverage. It has all the benefits of soymilk and an added flavor of smoky aroma from roasting.

1/2 pound dried split mung beans
   or yellow beans
2 tablespoons brown sugar
1 tablespoon margarine
1/8 teaspoon salt (optional)

Rinse the beans with cold water and set aside to dry. In a heavy skillet over medium heat, dry roast the beans 7–8 minutes or until light brown. Add the sugar, margarine, and optional salt and stir to mix well. Remove from the heat and let cool.

Process the beans in a grinder until they are the consistency of coffee grounds. Brew like fresh-ground coffee, and serve with sugar and cream (the same way you would serve a cup of coffee). It can also be served cold over ice.

Sticky Rice Wrapped Banana

Serves 6 (makes 12 pieces)

Khao Tom Mud

In contrast to the jasmine rice that is usually served with Thai savory dishes, sticky rice is stickier, sweeter, and, in addition to being eaten plain like the jasmine rice, often is used in Thai desserts. Very ripe and sweet Thai bananas are a perfect filling and turn out well with the steaming technique.

2 cups sweet sticky long-grain rice [*khao neaw*]

¼ cup dried black beans

1 cup coconut cream

1 cup sugar

½ teaspoon salt

6 ripe Thai bananas [*kluai nam wa*], or 12 baby bananas [*kluai khai*], or 3 regular bananas

1 bunch banana leaves, cut into 24 pieces, each about 8 x 10 inches

½ cup shredded coconut, for garnish

Soak the rice and black beans separately in cold water to cover for at least 3 hours or overnight. Drain well.

Combine the rice, coconut cream, ¾ cup of the sugar, and ¼ teaspoon of the salt in a medium saucepan over medium heat. Simmer, stirring occasionally, until the rice has absorbed all the liquid. Make sure that the rice does not burn on the bottom of the saucepan. The mixture should be fairly dry and gluey and hold together loosely. Remove from the heat and let cool.

Place the beans in a medium saucepan with 2 cups of fresh water. Bring to a boil, reduce the heat, cover, and simmer until the beans are tender and can be mashed between your fingers. Do not overcook the beans. Drain and set aside.

Peel the bananas, slice in half lengthwise, and cut into 3½-inch-long pieces.

To make a wrapper, use two pieces of banana leaves, one on top of the other with the grains crossing. Spread some of the rice mixture thinly at the center of a wrapper, a little larger than the size of a sliced banana. Place a piece of banana at the center of the rice and top with more rice to cover the banana completely. Sprinkle with the cooked black beans. Pull the edges of the wrapper together and then fold and wrap the contents tightly into a log with both ends tucked underneath. Continue wrapping until all rice and bananas have been used.

Arrange the wrapped bananas on a steamer rack over boiling water and steam over high heat for 45–50 minutes or until the rice is fully cooked.

Combine the shredded coconut, the remaining ¼ cup of sugar, and the remaining ¼ teaspoon salt in a bowl. Mix well.

Serve the stuffed banana as it is, warm or at room temperature (do not eat the banana leaves). Alternatively, unwrap and slice the filling into bite-size pieces. Sprinkle with the shredded coconut mixture.

Tapioca Pudding with Tropical Fruits

Serves 6

Saku Paek

Tapioca lovers will be in heaven, as this is their kind of dessert. The unique texture and creamy flavor of tapioca and coconut cream bring out the vibrancy of a tropical fruit medley. Warm or cold, this dessert is quite hearty and satisfying after a spicy Thai meal.

2 cups water

1/2 cup small pearl tapioca

1/2 cup fruit syrup from preserved fruits

1 1/2 cups coconut cream (1 cup for pudding, and 1/2 cup for topping)

1 cup sugar (3/4 cup for pudding, and 1/4 cup for topping)

1 teaspoon pandan, jasmine, or vanilla extract

1 1/2 cups sliced assorted tropical fruit (a combination of fresh and preserved)

1 tablespoon cornstarch

1/4 teaspoon salt

1 bunch orchid flowers or rose petals, for garnish

Bring the water to a boil in a medium saucepan. Add the tapioca, stirring constantly. Reduce the heat and simmer for 10–15 minutes or until all the tapioca pearls are soft and clear. Stir in the fruit syrup.

Stir in 1 cup of the coconut cream, ¾ cup of the sugar, and the pandan extract. Simmer until the sugar is fully dissolved. Remove from the heat and stir in the sliced fruits. Reserve some of the fruits for a garnish.

Combine the remaining ½ cup coconut cream, remaining ¼ cup sugar, cornstarch, and salt in a medium saucepan. Cook over medium heat until thickened to a gravy-like consistency. Remove from the heat and set aside for later use as a topping.

Ladle the tapioca pudding into individual serving bowls and spread the topping over the surface. Garnish with extra sliced fruit and orchid flowers just before serving. Serve warm or cold.

Sweet Corn and Coconut

Serves 6

Simplicity is the key to this dessert, but fresh ingredients, from fresh corn to fresh coconut, are essential in order to achieve its characteristic refreshing taste. Frozen corn and canned products are not worth the effort.

3–4 ears of fresh sweet corn, shucked

1 fresh ripe coconut

$1/3 - 1/2$ cup sugar

$1/2$ teaspoon salt

1 cup julienne jackfruit (optional)

2 tablespoons roasted black sesame seeds

Cook the corn in boiling water for 5–7 minutes or until tender. Using a sharp knife, cut the kernels off the cobs to make at least 3 cups of kernels.

Crack open the coconut with a hammer or the back of a sturdy cleaver. Discard the juice and shred the white meat into fine strands to make at least 1 cup of shredded coconut. Combine the coconut, sugar, and salt in a bowl. Add the corn kernels and optional jackfruit. Mix well and transfer to a serving platter. Garnish with the roasted sesame seeds.

Taro Cakes

Serves 6

Taro has developed a bad reputation in the West as being as tasteless and gluey as wallpaper paste; it's also often incorrectly associated with Hawaiian poi. In fact, taro has a distinctive taste and aroma that is perfectly suited for sweets. In this recipe, with a slow-cooking reduction method, the taste and flavor of taro are more intense and most desirable.

2 pounds fresh taro roots

2 cups coconut cream

1 1/4 cups palm sugar

3/4 teaspoon salt

2 teaspoons pandan, jasmine, rose, or vanilla extract

Wash the taro roots with cold water. Cook in boiling water or steam in a steamer for 10–15 minutes or until tender and the skins peel off easily. Let cool and peel the skins completely. Alternatively, peel the raw taro roots completely and cut into small chunks. Boil in plenty of water to cover until tender. Do not overcook to the point that they are disintegrated. Drain well.

Transfer the cooked taro to a food processor and process into a fine paste. Add the coconut cream, palm sugar, pandan extract, and salt. Process just until well combined.

Transfer the mixture to a deep pot or pan (copper is preferred for its even distribution of heat), and cook and stir over medium heat for 30–35 minutes or until dry, thick, and gluey and no longer sticking to the pan.

Transfer to a 10-inch-square pan or tray at least 2 inches deep. Smooth and level the surface. Let cool. Cut into pieces any size or shape of your choice.

Thai Cupcakes

Serves 6 (makes 30 pieces)

These little sweets are the true Thai dessert without any foreign influences. Little, inexpensive ceramic cups, called "tuay talai," were invented for this dessert of basic ingredients: rice flour, sugar, and coconut. Steaming is the age-old method that is prevalent in Thai cooking.

BOTTOM LAYER:

2 teaspoons jasmine or pandan extract

1 cup water

1 1/2 cups coconut milk

1 1/2 cups sugar

3/4 cup rice flour

30 small saucers, 2 inches in diameter and at least 1/2 inch deep

TOP LAYER:

2 cups coconut cream

1/4 cup rice flour

1/2 teaspoon salt

Dilute the jasmine extract in the water in a medium bowl to make jasmine water. Add the coconut milk, sugar, and flour, and stir until the sugar is dissolved.

Arrange 30 small saucers in a steamer rack over high heat, and cover with a tight-fitting lid. Heat the saucers for 3–5 minutes. Pour the mixture into the heated saucers, filling each about three-quarters full. Cook 6–7 minutes or until firm.

Combine all the top layer ingredients in a small bowl and stir to mix well. Pour on top of the cooked bottom layers to almost fill the saucers. Continue cooking in the steamer 6–7 minutes longer or until the top layers are firm.

To serve, run a small blade around the saucers to loosen the cupcakes. Turn the saucers over on a serving platter and shake to remove the cupcakes. Alternatively, serve directly in the container, warm or at room temperature.

Thai Iced Tea

Serves 6

When naming popular Thai drinks, Thai iced tea [cha yen] is the first choice. The blend of Thai tea imparts a complex flavor of herbs and spices. This recipe excludes the animal products milk and cream for a rather refreshing iced tea drink. Thai tea is a blend of tea leaves, herbs, and spices that is sold under the name "Thai Seasoning Mix" or "Cha Thai." It is available in one-pound packages in well-stocked Asian grocery stores.

8 cups water

1/2 – 3/4 cup Cha Thai or Thai Seasoning Mix

3/4 cup sugar, more or less to taste

4 cups crushed ice

6 wedges of lime or lemon

Bring the water to a boil in a large pot. Add the tea and simmer for 10 minutes. Strain the tea through a fine sieve; save the liquid and discard the solids. Add the sugar and stir until dissolved. Chill in the refrigerator.

To serve, fill a tall serving glass with crushed ice. Pour the tea over the ice and squeeze a wedge of lime or lemon; stir well.

Resources

Chompituk, Yuvadee. *Arhan Thai See Phak*. Bangkok: Rungsang Printing, 1998.

Cilinaria Konemann. *Southeast Asian Specialties*. Cologne: Konemann, 1998.

Davidson, Alan. *The Penguin Companion to Food*. New York: Penguin Group, 2002.

Gruenwald, Joerg. *PDR for Herbal Medicines*. Montcale: Medical Economic Company Inc., 1998.

Herbst, Sharon Tyler. *The New Food Lover's Companion*. New York: Barron's Educational Series, Inc., 2001.

Heymann-Sukpan, Wanphen. *The Foods of Thailand*. New York: U.S. Media Holdings Inc., 1996.

Holzen, Heinz von. *The Food of Indonesia*. Singapore: Periplus Editions (HK) Ltd., 1999.

Kongpun, Sisamon. *The Best of Thai Dishes*. Bangkok: Sangdad Books, 2000.

Mahidol University. *The Miracle of Veggies 108*. Bangkok: Kopfai Publishing, 1997.

Mcnair, James. *Cooks Southeast Asia*. San Francisco: Chronicle Books, 1996.

Mingkwan, Chat. *The Best of Regional Thai Cuisine*. New York: Hippocrene Books, 2002.

Owen, Sri. *Classic Asian*. London: DK Publishing Inc., 1998.

Poladitmontri, Panurat. *The Thai Beautiful Cookbook*. San Francisco: Collins Publishers, 1992.

Sawedvimon, Sunti. *Tumnan Arhan Thai*. Bangkok: Nanmeebooks, 1999.

Thanakit. *50 Nitan Thai*. Bangkok: Sureewiyasarn Printing, 1996.

Thonanong, Thongyao. *Royal Court Recipes*. Bangkok: Sangdad Books, 1998.

Walden, Hilary. *The Encyclopedia of Creative Cuisine*. London: Quarto Publishing Limited, 1986.

Yu, Su-Mei. *Cracking The Coconut*. New York: Harper Collins Publishers Inc., 2000.

Mail Order/Online Retailers

Thai food has become very popular in recent years. Ingredients for making Thai food at home can be found in local Asian markets. You also can conveniently shop on the Internet. Just type "Thai ingredients" into a search engine and you'll find over one hundred Web sites and online retailers related to Thai food and ingredients. Here are a few good places to start:

To find Thai markets near you:

> www.thaitable.com

For online retailers:

> www.templeofthai.com

> www.importfood.com

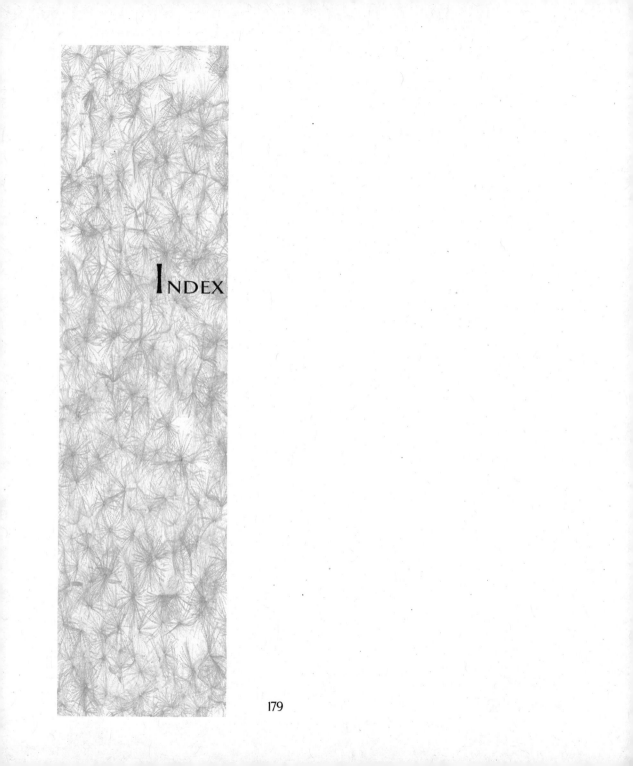

INDEX

ingredients for Thai cooking 13-34
   See also specific ingredient listings
I-teem Kati 158

J
jackfruit 28
jasmine 24, 154
jasmine rice 31
Jelly, Pandan 166-167
jicama 28
Jub Chay 88

K
kabocha 28
kaffir lime 9, 24, 130
Kalum Yud Sai 80
kamin 25
kana 26
kanom
   Bueng Yuan 58-59
   Cheen Nam Ngew 136
   Cheen Nam Ya 134-135
   jeen 32
   Kluai 156
   Tuay 175
kanon 28
kati 27
kecap 14
kha 23
khao 30-31
   gong 30-31
   hoam mali 31
   Kreong Tead 152
   Mun Kati 133
   neaw 31

neaw dum 31
Neaw Mamoung 168
Pad 104
phot awn 25-26
Pood Kruk 173
Pood Tod 55
Tom King 95
Tom Mud 170-171
Yum 78-79
kheun chai 26
Khun toke 8
Kluai Buat Chee 155
Kra Pro Pla 90-91
kra-chai 24
kuai-tiao 31-32
Kuay Teow Pad Se-iew 122-123
Kuay Teow Rad Na 126
kui chay 23-24

L
Laab Hed 71
Laab Tou Hu 72
lemon basil 21
lemongrass 9, 24, 130
Lemongrass and Mushroom Salad 70
lesser ginger 24
lily bud or flower 28
lin chee 29
long beans 29
Long Bean Wrapped Mushrooms
   140-141
long eggplant 28
longan 29
luk kravan 22

ABOUT THE AUTHOR

As the youngest boy in an urban family in Bangkok, Chat Mingkwan was often left behind to help his aunt prepare the family dinner while his older brothers and sisters ran off to play. At first he despised the task of cooking, but he later learned to enjoy the knowledge and skills he gained, including discovering the sweet revenge of spiking and over-spicing his brother's and sisters' meals. Chat often intentionally prepared their meals with almost unbearable spiciness and got away with it. The food was so spicy but still so delicious that Chat's siblings were unsure whether to punish or praise him. Eventually, cooking became his passion. He gradually fine-tuned his skills and continued cooking, although praise was his only reward and encouragement.

Chat came to the United States to pursue higher education in a design field, while cooking and training part time in a French restaurant as a hobby. This was his first big step in the culinary profession. With a degree from California State University, Chat worked for several years in the hospitality design business, specializing in kitchen and restaurant design. Later, he followed his yearning culinary passion by apprenticing at La Cagouille in provincial French cuisine in

Rayon, France. Returning to the United States, he offered his French cooking always with a twist of Thai and perfected his Thai cooking with a hint of French techniques to fit the Western kitchen. Chat traveled extensively throughout Southeast Asia and realized a wealth of culinary knowledge among these countries and their unique cuisines. He again became an apprentice, this time of Southeast Asian cuisine, and easily mastered the skill with his Thai cooking background. Chat put his skills to the test for several years in the culinary metropolis of San Francisco at a restaurant that specialized in Southeast Asian grilled food before realizing his call for sharing the knowledge. He's now doing what he likes most: cooking, teaching, traveling, writing, and making sure that people who come in contact with him have a full stomach and a good time.

Chat's overall philosophy is similar to his cooking simplicity. Untie the knot, either the one in your stomach or the unclear one in the recipe. Make it simple, straight, and true to yourself. Let's walk this path together.

Visit Chat at www.unusualtouch.com; there is something for everyone.

Introduction

BOOK PUBLISHING COMPANY

since 1974—books that educate, inspire, and empower

To find your favorite vegetarian and soyfood products online, visit:
www.healthy-eating.com

Coconut Oil for Health and Beauty
Cynthia Holzapfel
Laura Holzapfel
978-1-57067-158-6 $9.95 US

The New Now and Zen Epicure
Miyoko Nishimoto Schinner
978-1-57067-114-2 $19.95 US

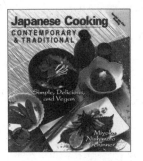

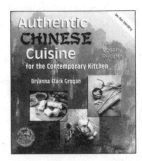

Japanese Cooking:
Contemporary & Traditional
Miyoko Nishimoto Schinner
978-1-57067-072-5 $12.95 US

Flavors of Korea
Young Sook Ramsay
and Deborah Davis
978-1-57067-053-4 $12.95 US

Authentic Chinese Cuisine
for the Contemporary Kitchen
Bryanna Clark Grogan
978-1-57067-101-2 $12.95 US

Purchase these health titles and cookbooks from your local bookstore or
natural food store, or you can buy them directly from:

Book Publishing Company • P.O. Box 99 • Summertown, TN 38483
1-800-695-2241

Please include $3.95 per book for shipping and handling.